True Indian Stories

MŬK-KŌNS-KWĂ, OR LITTLE BEAR WOMAN.
(Frances Slocum—The Lost Sister of Wyoming.)

TRUE
INDIAN STORIES

WITH

GLOSSARY OF INDIANA
INDIAN NAMES

BY

JACOB PIATT DUNN
SECRETARY OF THE INDIANA HISTORICAL SOCIETY

SENTINEL PRINTING COMPANY
INDIANAPOLIS, INDIANA

1909

341994

CONTENTS

CHAPTER   PAGE

I   INTRODUCING THE INDIANS   I

II   THE LITTLE TURTLE   15

III   THE DEATH OF THE WITCHES   48

IV   WHY TECUMTHA FOUGHT   72

V   THE FALL OF THE PROPHET   93

VI   WILLIAM WELLS   117

VII   THE DEFENSE OF FORT HARRISON   131

VIII   THE PIGEON ROOST MASSACRE   144

IX   THE SERVICE OF LOGAN   164

X   THE WALAM OLUM   181

XI   THE TRAGEDY OF THE FALLS   197

XII   THE LOST SISTER OF WYOMING   213

XIII   THE TRAIL OF DEATH   234

INDEX GLOSSARY OF INDIANA INDIAN NAMES   253

ILLUSTRATIONS

	PAGE
FRANCES SLOCUM	Frontispiece
GABRIEL GODFROY . .	8
SITE OF FORT WAYNE IN 1790	21
GREENVILLE TREATY MEDAL	39
KILSOKWA . . .	46
DELAWARE COUNCIL HOUSE	55
SITE OF WHITE RIVER MISSION	63
TECUMTHA	80
MAP OF INDIANA IN 1811	87
TEMSKWAHTAWAH	facing 94
PLAN OF BATTLE OF TIPPECANOE	105
THE PROPHET'S ROCK	109
WILLIAM WELLS.... ..	118
MAP OF CHICAGO IN 1812	121
FORT DEARBORN MASSACRE MONUMENT	129
SITE OF FORT HARRISON	134
DEFENSE OF FORT HARRISON	141
MAP OF PIGEON ROOST SETTLEMENT	146
PIGEON ROOST MONUMENT	157
FORT WAYNE IN 1812	167
BLACK HOOF . . .	175
ILLUSTRATION OF SIGN LANGUAGE	183
SAMPLE PAGE OF WALAM OLUM	190
THE FALLS AT PENDLETON	207
ROCK BLUFFS ON THE MISSISSINEWA	215
THE DEAF MAN'S VILLAGE .	223
THE FRANCES SLOCUM MONUMENT	231
FOOT OF NASWAWKEE'S HILL	237
SITE OF MISSION AT TWIN LAKES	245
THE DESCENT OF MONDAMIN	262
METEAH	279
SITE OF POST OUIATANON . . .	294
MAP OF TREATY SPRINGS . .	311

TRUE INDIAN STORIES

CHAPTER I.

INTRODUCING THE INDIANS.

No part of the United States is richer in the tragedy, romance and pathos of Indian history than the region included in the old Territory Northwest of the Ohio River. It might be called the empire of the Algonquian tribes within our boundaries; for although they extended far into British America; although there was a large detached tribe—the Blackfeet—in the West; although the Lenni Lenape reached away to the Atlantic coast, most of the Algonquians of the United States were here at the earliest known period, and the Eastern tribes were thrown back here as settlement progressed. It was here that they made their last stand for their country east of the Mississippi and put the white man to his best effort to conquer them. No part of the country ever produced greater Indians than Pontiac, Tecumtha, The Little Turtle, Pŏch-gŏnt'-shē-hē-lŏs, and Black Hawk.

When the French entered this region their first task was to aid the resident tribes in driving back the Iroquois, who had acquired firearms, and had almost overrun the country to the Mississippi. After this was done there was comparative peace until individual tribes undertook war against the French; but the French were always able to hold the alliance of most of the tribes, and by their aid almost exterminated the Mascoutins at Detroit in 1712, and the Foxes in northern Illinois in 1730. The French always treated the Indians well and made notable efforts for their spiritual welfare as well as for their temporal needs. It was chiefly to a missionary enterprise that Indiana's first permanent settlement was due. Father De Beaubois, the priest at Kaskaskia, and in charge of the religious interests of the Illinois settlements, desired to extend his work by the establishment of a post on the Wabash and an assembling of Indians there. He gained the approval of the Louisiana authorities, who also desired an additional supply of clergy and an establishment of nuns, of whom there were none in Louisiana at the time.

In 1725 De Beaubois was sent to France on this mission. The Chevalier de Bourgmont had collected twenty-two chiefs and representative Indians to accompany him, but just before they were to embark the ship in which they were going sank at its moorings, and this so frightened them that only half a dozen of the Indians could be induced to make the journey. Their visit in France was as notable an event in the world of fashion as the visit of Pocahontas to England, and the account of their presentation at the court and attendant celebrations fills thirty-three pages of the court journal, Le Mercure de France. De Beaubois succeeded in his undertaking and sent out to Louisiana the nuns who founded the celebrated Ursuline Convent at New Orleans, and with them Father D'Outreleau, who was to be the first "Missionary to the Ouabache." Orders were also sent for the establishment of a post. The contemplated mission did not succeed; but in the summer of 1731 Sieur de Vincennes brought a small party of soldiers and a band of Piankeshaws from the Vermillion River and founded the post which still bears his name.

By this time the efforts of the English to get control of the fur trade had become more serious, and they, too, had enlisted Indian allies both in the north and in the south. First came the disastrous Chickasaw campaign of 1736, in which Vincennes lost his life; and after that intermittent warfare till the close of the French and Indian war. In all this the fighting was outside of our region, and not till the British sought to take possession of the Northwest was it brought back in Pontiac's war. Again there was comparative quiet until the war of the Revolution, which inaugurated the contest of the American and the Indian in this section for the occupancy of the soil. Of the period then beginning I have sought to present some authentic stories in the following pages. It would require volumes to present a full record of individual adventure, but I have aimed to give some illustrations of various phases of the contest, of battles and massacres, of hardships, of white and Indian captivity.

In doing this I have had especially in

mind the preservation of the Indian names of Indiana in their proper forms and with their real meanings. This will be regarded by many as a presumptuous undertaking, and with some reason. Several months ago, in a letter to me concerning Indian place names, Gen. R. H. Pratt, of Carlisle School fame, said: "The subject has not specially interested me for the reason that, in my experience, not one in twenty of the Indian names in use could be recognized by any member of the tribe from which the name was derived. The attempts to perpetuate such names are therefore only sentimental abortion." This is very true, and true of Indiana names as well as of those elsewhere, but there is no question of perpetuating the names. They are here to stay. In the defiant words of Mrs. Sigourney—

"Their name is on your waters—
Ye may not wash it out."

And nobody desires to wash them out. That were a waste of energy much better directed to washing something else. The practical question is merely whether we shall continue their use without an effort to ascertain their origin and meaning. As to this,

5

the extent of their corruption seems to me an attraction rather than an objection. Nobody cares much for a puzzle that is readily solved, in philology or in any other line. But there is at least passing interest in identifying any battered and distorted relic; and in reality our Indian names are no more corrupted than some others. Probably no Frenchman would be reminded of his native tongue by "Picketwire," but that is what the cowboys of Colorado and New Mexico have made of the Purgatoire River. Probably no Frenchman would suspect the Smackover River of Arkansas of bearing a French name, but that is what remains of "Chemin Couvert." Our own Mary Delome has rather a French air, but hardly enough to suggest that this tributary of the Maumee was named "Marais de l'Orme" (Elm Swamp). On some of our maps of Laporte County will be found "Lake Dishmaugh," which does not look much like French, but it was originally "Lac du Chemin," though Chamberlain made the guess that it had been "Lac des Moines."

Surely no Hindoo would lay claim to "Indiana" as of his language, but it is from the same root as "Hindoo" itself, for it comes from "Sindhu," the native name of the Indus—literally "the river"—whence Sindh or Scinde, the province covering the delta. This the Persians perverted to "Hindu"; the Greeks made it "Indos"; the Romans "Indus," and from them it passed to the various European forms. When Columbus discovered America he supposed it was India; hence, he called the natives "Indios"; and the name has abided. At the treaty of Ft. Stanwix, in 1768, the Indians ceded a tract of land in western Pennsylvania to certain traders, whose goods they had taken or destroyed; and for this tract and for the company organized to exploit it, the name "Indiana" was evolved by the English owners. It is constructed on the same principle as Florida, Georgia, Virginia, etc., and means a place of Indians, or pertaining to Indians. This name was passed on to us when Ohio was cut off from Northwest Territory in 1800; but in the name of "Indiana County," Pennsylvania, it still appears at the place of its birth.

As a matter of fact there is usually no great difficulty in ascertaining the real In-

GABRIEL GODFROY.
(Wah'-pah-nah-ki'-kah-pwah—or White Blossoms.)

dian name if it is of a living language, for the Indians usually perpetuate their own names, though occasionally they have their own corruptions. Most of the Miami names I obtained from Gabriel Godfroy, the best Miami interpreter in Indiana, and Kilsokwa, the oldest of the Indiana Miamis, and one who speaks very little English. For the Pota watomi I am indebted to Thomas Topash, an intelligent Potawatomi of Michigan; Quashma, a Chilocco School boy, and Capt. J. A. Scott, of Nadeau Agency, Kansas, who called to his aid Mr. Blandin, the agency interpreter, and old Kack-kack (Kiăk-kiăk— equivalent to the American term, "chickenhawk"; i. e., any of the larger hawks), recently deceased. For others I am indebted largely to various friends who made inquiry of Indians.

It is much to be regretted that there is not in print more available information concerning the Indian languages, and especially of the Algonquian languages, from which so many of our place names are taken. There is considerable material for the Odjibwa and the dialects of the Lenni Lenape, but scarcely anything for the languages of the important

9

Potawatomi, Shawnee and Miami nations,
and what little there is is not entirely relia-
ble. And this is true of many other Indian
languages. At the last session of Congress
(1907-8) the Indiana Historical Society
made an earnest effort to secure a small additional appropriation for the Bureau of
Ethnology for taking up systematically and
specially the preservation of these languages, but notwithstanding the co-operation of the Bureau, the appropriation was re-
jected by the House, after it had been made
by the Senate. There should unquestionably
be an united effort by the historical societies
of the country to have this work done. When
we consider the enormous effort that has
been made to rescue the languages of Egypt,
Babylon and other ancient countries, it
should arouse a realization of the importance
of preserving the living languages of our
own country while there is yet time, and
especially so because these are not written
languages, and if once lost they are lost forever.

And they are worth preserving, not only
for the influence they have had on our own
language, but for their intrinsic merit.

Nearly all of our common errors as to Indian names are due to the prevalent impression that Indian languages are very crude. In reality they have a very perfect grammatical system of their own, but differing in important features from that of any other known languages. The grammatical inflections of Algonquian words are more refined and present nicer distinctions of meaning, not only than those of the English, but also than those of any European language. If anyone doubts this statement I would refer him to the conjugation of the verb "waub" of the Odjibwa, as given by Schoolcraft in his "Archives," covering ninety quarto pages; and this is not complete, because it does not cover what are known as the "transitions," i. e., the combinations with subject and object pronouns, which are characteristic of these languages. And yet, complicated as this might seem, it is on a very simple and rational linguistic system, and simply expresses through verbal inflection the same ideas that we express through various forms of circumlocution.

I doubt that anyone has ever reproduced exactly the Indian pronunciation of words.

All of the Algonquian languages have some sounds that are not found in the English language, and none of them have all of the English sounds. In addition to this they all have interchangeable sounds. For example, the sounds of "b" or "p" may be used at the will of the speaker in many words. Moreover, there is an emphasis and accent that white men rarely acquire—in fact, I have never found an Indian who knew a white man that could speak his language just as the Indians speak it. However, I have endeavored to reproduce Indian pronunciation, as it sounds to me, as nearly as possible in ordinary English characters, with a few additions. I have represented long "a" as in "fate" by "ay"; continental "a" as in "far" by "ah;" and broad "a" as in "fall" by "aw." I have used "q" to represent a sound more nearly resembling German "ch" than any other I know of, but having the quality of "gh," pronounced in the same way. Nasalized sounds are indicated by a superior "n," and are pronounced as in the French.

If the effort I have been able to give to the subject shall promote the study and record of the Indian languages, I shall feel largely repaid for it, for the opportunity for this work is rapidly decreasing. In our governmental Indian schools the study of Indian languages is not encouraged, and perhaps properly so, from a practical point of view, for the primary object is to fit the Indian youth to support themselves, and for this the use of the English language is vital. It is already quite common to find "educated Indians" who do not speak their own language at all, and obviously the more rapid the process of "Americanizing" the more rapid the extinction of the American languages. It is, therefore, evident that the work should be undertaken as speedily as possible.

Prior to this time there have been two efforts at collecting Indian place names of Indiana. In his Indiana Gazetteer (1849) Mr. Chamberlain has noted a number of Delaware names, which were presumably obtained from white men who had some familiarity with the Delaware language. There were several of such persons in the State at the time. Later Daniel Hough made a more extended effort and collected nearly everything then available in print, as well as making some investigations among the Miami

Indians. The results were published in the Geological Report of 1882 in the form of a map, with comments by Judge Hiram Beckwith. The comments are of no practical value, being chiefly attempts to deduce Miami and Potawatomi words from Odjibwa stems, but the map is of material value, although Mr. Hough's patient work has been marred in several instances by mistakes of the engraver.

CHAPTER II.

THE LITTLE TURTLE.

The greatest of the Miamis and, perhaps, by the standard of achievement, which is the fairest of all standards, the greatest Indian the world has known, was Mi'-shi-kin-nŏq'-kwa, commonly known as The Little Turtle, but that is not what his name means. Literally it means The Great Turtle's Wife, but it is not in that sense that it was applied to this great chief.

The Miamis have specific names for the most common turtles—ăt-chē'-pŏng for the snapping turtle, ah-koot'-yah for the soft-shell turtle, wē-nēēt'-chah for the box turtle or tortoise, kăch-kĭt'-yŏt for the map turtle, and mi-shi-kin-nŏq'-kwa for the painted terrapin. This last is the commonest of all the turtles in this region, and the most gaudily colored, which probably explains its Indian name, for who should be handsomely dressed if not the wife of The Great Turtle, who typi-

fied the Earth, and who was the chief beneficent manitou of the Algonquian tribes in the
olden time? But when it came to translation
the interpreters knew no specific English
name for the painted terrapin, and, as it is a
little turtle, never growing more than six or
eight inches across, they conveyed the idea as
well as they could by saying "The Little
Turtle."

The Little Turtle was rather small of stature, and was probably a puny infant, which
may account for his name, for a more
sprawling, helpless-looking creature than a
newly hatched painted terrapin can hardly be
imagined. It has been stated that his mother
was a Mohegan woman, but his granddaughter Kil-sō'-kwă (The Setting Sun) says that
both his father and his mother were full-
blooded Miamis. He was born near the present city of Ft. Wayne, about 1751. Though
small of stature, he was both brave and wise.
He had also a remarkable dignity of manner
that commanded respect, and although not a
hereditary chief, he soon rose to a position of
leadership. His first opportunity for special
distinction came in 1780.

Up to that time the region about the headwaters of the Maumee had not been disturbed in the war with the Americans, but had been a center, easy of access to the British, from which supplies were distributed and warriors were sent out to harass the frontiers. It had been an Indian stronghold for many years. Before the Miamis dwelt there it was occupied by the Ottawas, or Pierced Noses—so called because they punctured the cartilage of the nose, as women do their ears, and suspended ornaments from it—and the Maumee was in early times known as the Ottawa River.

At the site of Ft. Wayne was the town of one of their clans or divisions, who were called Kis-kǎ-kǒns or Ki-kǎ-kǒns, i. e., Clipped Hair, or as the French called them, Queues Coupees, because they shaved the sides of their heads and wore their hair in a bristling band across the head from front to back. This name always attached to the place, but the Delawares corrupted it to Kē-gey-ūnk, which would mean "old place" if it meant anything, and the Miamis to Kē-ki-oon'-gi, which would mean "cut place" if it meant anything, but both tribes disclaim knowledge of the meaning of these names, which is very proper because they lost the real meaning long ago. Here and at smaller villages in the vicinity the Miamis had dwelt for nearly a century in apparent security.

But in 1780 a rude shock occurred. Out from the East there came Colonel Le Balme, a French officer, who came over with Lafayette and had been serving with the Continental army in New England. Inspired perhaps by the success of George Rogers Clark, he conceived a plan for capturing Detroit with a force raised in the French settlements. He won the confidence of the French settlers on the Mississippi, and thirty of them started with him on his expedition. At Vincennes he recruited nearly as many more.

The expedition was well managed in the earlier part. The men were mounted, and they passed up the Wabash quickly and quietly, making the journey from the Wea towns in four days, and taking Kē-ki-oon'-gi by surprise. There were few Indians in the town and they fled, as did the British traders, most of whom were of French birth. The invaders took some plunder from the stores and then fell back to the Aboite River, where they encamped in fancied security. But they counted without their host.

The alarm spread rapidly and soon came to The Little Turtle, who quickly gathered a band of warriors to attack the enemy. Finding Kē-ki-oon′-gi abandoned, they followed back the trail and in the darkness of the night struck the sleeping camp. La Balme had not even posted sentinels, and he and his men were all killed except a young man named Rhy, who was carried captive to Canada and handed over to the British authorities. He said he was aid-de-camp to La Balme, and that they had fallen back to the Aboite to await reinforcements to the number of 400, which were expected, but of these nothing further was ever heard. The news of the destruction of the expedition against Detroit was received with great satisfaction by the British, and thenceforth The Little Turtle was the recognized war chief of the Miamis.

It has been surmised by local historians that the Aboite received its name from this event, the original form being Abattoir, which was later corrupted to the present form. This is wholly unfounded, as the stream is called Riviere a Boite in documents

and maps of earlier date. Boitte, or its vari-
ant bouette, is a word used by French fishermen for minnows that are used as bait for
larger fish and their name for the stream was
River of Minnows. The Miamis call it Nă-
kŏw'-ē-sē'-pē, or Sand Creek.

In the next ten years there was an abund-
ance of fighting, of Indian raids on the Kentucky settlements and all along the frontier,
with counter expeditions by the whites. It
has been estimated that between the close of
the Revolutionary war and 1790 the Indians
killed 1,500 people and ran off 20,000 horses.
They did the greater damage, but they were
being gradually forced back and losing their
old homes. Many retired to the Miami country, and in 1785 Kē-ki-oon'-gi is said to have
had a population of 1,000 warriors of various
tribes. But the white man was growing
weary of this petty and harassing warfare,
and this feeling was increased by the belief,
supported by very convincing evidence, that
the British, who still held the region about
Detroit, were furnishing supplies to the Indians and urging them to war. It was decided that a crushing blow must be struck,
and in 1790 an expedition was started

VIEW OF THE MAUMEE TOWNS

DESTROYED BY GENERAL HARMAR

October 1790

DELAWARES

SHAWANEES

PRINCIPAL TOWN OF
MIAMIS & SHAWANEES

MIAMIS

against the Miami town under command of Gen. Josiah Harmar, the commander-in-chief of the American army.

The expedition consisted of 1,453 men, rank and file, of whom 320 were regulars and the remainder militia and volunteers from Pennsylvania, Virginia and Kentucky. But the latter were not up to the frontier standard. Many were boys and old men, and most of them were poorly equipped. They were almost without discipline, and showed a great deal of insubordination. There was jealousy among the officers that extended to the men. Nevertheless, the army moved forward. The advance guard of 600 men, under Col. Hardin, reached Kē-ki-oon'-gi on October 15, and the remainder of the army two days later. They found the place deserted. Most of the men were away on their fall hunt and the rest had hastily retired.

On the 18th Colonel Trotter was sent out with 300 men, thirty of whom were regulars, to look for Indians, while the remainder of the force engaged in the destruction of the villages and crops. Trotter's trip was unsuccessful, and on the 19th Colonel Hardin was sent out with the same command. The

Indians were not strong enough to attack the main army, but The Little Turtle had collected one hundred warriors and he placed them in ambush some ten miles northwest of Kē-ki-oon'-gi when Hardin was reported coming. Hardin marched into the ambush and the Indians opened fire and advanced. All the militiamen except nine fled, and these, with the regulars, were quickly hemmed in and subjected to a pitiless fire, from which only one escaped to tell the tale.

On the same day the army left Kē-ki-oon'-gi and moved two miles down the Maumee to a Shawnee town, where the work of destruction was kept up. On the 21st, having destroyed five villages and 20,000 bushels of corn, with quantities of beans, pumpkins, hay and fencing, the army started on its return and marched eight miles south. That night, at the request of Hardin, who desired to retrieve his misfortune of the 19th, Harmar sent back a force of four hundred men under his command, of whom sixty were regulars under Major Wyllis.

The detachment marched in three divisions a few hundred yards apart, intending to surprise the Indians, who, it was anticipated, would return to their villages early in the morning. But The Little Turtle was not surprised. A small force of Indians appeared before the right wing and when attacked fled up the St. Joseph, which the Miamis called Kō-chis-ah-sē-pē, or Bean River, the division, contrary to orders, following them for several miles.

Then The Little Turtle, with his main force, fell on the center division, which included the regulars. The regulars fought bravely, but lost so heavily that they were forced to retire up the St. Joseph. They were on the east side of the stream and the Indians followed, mostly on the west side, pouring in a deadly fire from behind trees and other cover.

At last the remnant met the returning militia, and with their united forces they compelled the Indians to fall back, and the soldiers rejoined the left wing at Kē-ki-oon'-gi. From there they returned to the main army without pursuit, the regulars having lost two officers and forty-eight men and the total loss to the army now reaching 183 killed and missing, besides many wounded, a number of whom had to be carried on stretchers. Hardin desired Harmar to go back with the army, but a council of officers decided that it was in no condition to do so. The Indians had suffered large loss of property, but were left with the belief that they had driven the Americans back.

The expedition of Harmar was followed by renewed attacks all along the frontier, the Indians being inspired both by the desire for revenge and the necessity of obtaining supplies of food. A bitter cry went up from the settlers. The Ohio company voted to raise troops to protect its settlements. Virginia provided for military expeditions from Kentucky, which was then part of its domain.

Congress directed an expedition under General St. Clair, and the erection of forts in the Indian country to guarantee peace. The Kentucky expeditions against the Wabash towns were successful, and early in September St. Clair's forces moved northward about twenty-five miles from Fort Washington and erected Fort Hamilton, on the Great Miami River. On October 4 they advanced again, this time forty-two miles, and erected Fort Jefferson. On October 24 the army again advanced, and on November 3 reached a point on the headwaters of the Wabash near where Fort Recovery was afterward established.

The advance was much delayed by failure of the contractors to forward provisions, and the army was weakened by numerous desertions, and by sending back one of the best regiments in search of deserters. It now numbered about 2,000 men.

Meanwhile the Indians had been busy. They had been kept informed of the American plans as made public by their British friends and of the movements on the frontier as gathered by their own scouts. Efforts had been made to unite the tribes in sufficient force not only to repel invasion, but also to drive the whites from the region north of the Ohio. Foremost in these efforts were The Little Turtle, the Shawnee chief Blue Jacket (Wey'-ah-piēr-sĕn'-wah) and the great Delaware war chief known in our frontier literature as Buckongehelas (properly pronounced Pŏch-gŏnt'-shē-hē'-lŏs. Heckewelder writes it Pachgantschihilas and translates it "A fulfiller; one who succeeds in all he undertakes." This is figurative; literally it means "The Breaker to Pieces").

In the latter part of October these and

minor chiefs had gathered 1,400 warriors in the vicinity of Kē-ki-oon'-gi, and these assembled on the prairie, five miles below that place on the St. Marys River, which the Miamis called Mah-may'-i-wah-sē-pē'-way, or Sturgeon Creek, on account of the large number of sturgeon that used to run up it in the spawning season.

There was a division of sentiment as to who should have the chief command that threatened for a time to become serious. Some favored The Little Turtle and some Buckongehelas, but the latter was not a man to let personal consideration stand in the way of success. Dawson, who voiced General Harrison's opinion, said of him: "This man possessed all the qualities of a hero; no Christian knight was ever more scrupulous in performing all his engagements than the renowned Buckongehelas." He settled the controversy by withdrawing in favor of The Little Turtle on the ground that he was the younger and more active man.

And now The Little Turtle had no ordinary Indian foray on his hands. He had an army to deal with, and it must be handled as an army, for the Indians were determined not to await invasion and another destruction of their winter supplies. They must be furnished with food on their march to meet the enemy.

The Little Turtle divided his warriors into squads or messes of twenty each, and ordered that four from each mess, in rotation, should act as hunters for that mess for one day, bringing in at noon whatever game they had obtained. The commander was well informed as to the enemy. His scouts had hovered about the army for a month, stealing horses and cutting off stragglers at every opportunity. In the night of November 3 he brought his warriors close in around St. Clair's camp and prepared for the attack.

The Americans were summoned to arms for parade at daylight, as usual, and the waiting Indians silently watched their maneuvers. Half an hour before sunrise—near 6 o'clock—they were dismissed for breakfast, and as they dispersed to their quarters The Little Turtle gave the signal for attack. The militia outposts were quickly driven in, and the Indians pressed after, keeping under cover and maintaining a continuous rifle fire.

The troops were soon put in position and

discharged repeated volleys at their concealed foes, but with little effect. Charge
after charge was made, but the Indians nim-
bly retired before the bayonets and were back
again as soon as the soldiers turned, while a
destructive fire was poured into the charging
columns from the flanks. The Indians did
not show themselves except when raised by a
charge. They made special marks of the officers and artillerymen.

The fight was one-sided from the start,
and by half-past 3 o'clock the army was helpless. The artillery was silenced. The men
were huddling in the center of the camp, deaf
to orders. The Indians were closing in. Most
of the officers were dead, and those remaining saw that the only hope was in retreat. A
few brisk charges made an opening to the
road, and those who were able to go made
their way to it in utter rout. And as they fled
the panic seemed to grow. Fortunately the
Indians pursued for only four or five miles,
but the road for miles beyond that was
strewn with arms and accoutrements of men
who desired nothing to impede their flight.

The Little Turtle had vanquished an
American army 50 per cent. larger than his

own and had inflicted a loss of 37 officers and 593 men killed and 31 officers and 242 men wounded. He had captured all the enemy's artillery, camp equipage and supplies, valued at $32,800, besides much private property. He had blocked for the time being the invasion of his country.

This was the greatest victory ever gained by Indians over American troops. In the Sioux victories at Fort Kearny and on the Little Big Horn the Indians greatly outnumbered the whites. The Nez Perces, under Chief Joseph, met equal and superior forces of soldiers, but their successes were only defenses and skilful retreats. The only engagement comparable with the defeat of St. Clair was Braddock's defeat, and in that the Indians were aided and officered by Frenchmen, and would have retreated but for their officers, while the Americans were not allowed by Braddock to fight in their own way. The Little Turtle's victory was over a superior force, on its own chosen ground and was achieved wholly by Indian military skill.

The defeat of St. Clair was a fearful blow to the frontier settlements, most of which were at once abandoned, except those adjoin-

ing the forts. Nearly all the able-bodied settlers had gone to the front, and there was
mourning in nearly every family. The Indians were greatly emboldened, and war parties appeared all along the lines of the frontier, carrying havoc that brought forth a bitter cry for aid.

President Washington realized that more
adequate means must be taken to subdue the
Indians, and he asked Congress for authority
to raise three additional regiments of foot
and a squadron of horse. There was opposition to this in Congress on account of the
poverty of the country, and it was even proposed to abandon the Northwest Territory
and make the Ohio River the boundary of the
United States. But such sentiment was not
popular, and there was soon manifested a
widespread determination for adequate meas-
ures for conquering the Indians.

Congress provided for raising an army of
5,000 men, and President Washington called
"Mad Anthony" Wayne from his farm to
command it. Meanwhile every effort was
made to settle the trouble peacefully. Commissioners were sent to the Indians through
Canada, and councils were held, but the In-

dians stubbornly refused to treat except on condition that the Americans retire from north of the Ohio and make it the boundary between them.

Wayne went to Pittsburg in June, 1792, and began the work of organizing the army, but no offensive movements were made during that year, or until October, 1793, when he advanced to a point six miles beyond Ft. Jefferson and built Ft. Greenville. In December he sent a detachment forward which took possession of the field of St. Clair's defeat and established Ft. Recovery at that point. At these two posts Wayne wintered his army, and prepared for a sure blow in the coming summer.

Only one attack was made on Wayne's forces in 1793. On October 17 a train of twenty wagons, under convoy of two officers and ninety men, was attacked seven miles north of Ft. St. Clair. Most of the men fled, and the two officers and thirteen men who remained, were killed. The Indians captured seventy horses and took some of the supplies, but did not destroy the remainder.

The winter passed without material incident, Wayne drilling his troops and making everything ready, while the Indians were striving to bring other tribes to their aid. In this they were assisted by the British, especially those at the Roche de Bout (Rock of the End), a place at the lower end of the Maumee rapids, so called from a massive rock in the stream. Here the British had established a fort after the close of the Revolutionary war, far within the American lines, and here were located the storehouses of Colonel McKee, an Indian trader, who was one of the most obnoxious of the British agents in urging the Indians to war.

The Little Turtle appeared before Ft. Recovery on June 30 with a force of 1,500 men, a large number of whom were whites in disguise. They had expected to find the cannon they had captured from St. Clair and to use them in assaulting the fort, but they were disappointed. The Americans had discovered their hiding places, mostly under logs, and they were now mounted in the fort. But by chance they struck a convoy of ninety riflemen and fifty dragoons under Major McMahon, who were returning to the fort. They at once attacked and overwhelmed this force, killing five officers and seventeen men, wounding thirty, killing and wounding eighty-one horses and capturing 204. They then attacked the fort and continued their assault through most of the following day, but their rifles were of little effect and they withdrew.

A division of sentiment now arose among the Indians. They had found it impossible to surprise Wayne in camp, for his camps were always fortified by surrounding walls of logs and there was no opportunity to attack in the open except when the troops were ready for battle. The Little Turtle insisted that this was hopeless on account of Wayne's superior force; that it was useless to try to surprise "a chief who always slept with one eye open," and that the only way to fight him was to get in behind him and cut off his convoys, leaving him stranded in the wilderness. But they had succeeded only twice in striking convoys, and one of the successes was accidental. The British urged an attack on the army and promised aid. The Little Turtle was overruled and even accused of cowardice. The majority encouraged by their success with St. Clair, decided on a pitched battle and The Little

Turtle had no choice but submission to the decision.

General Scott on July 26 joined Wayne at Ft. Greenville with 1,600 mounted men from Kentucky, and on the 28th the army advanced. On August 8 they reached the Grand Glaize and proceeded to build Ft. Defiance at the junction of the Auglaize with the Maumee. On the 13th a prisoner was sent out with a peace message, advising the Indians to listen no longer to "the bad white men at the foot of the rapids," but to send peace deputies at once if they desired to save themselves and their women and children from famine and danger.

On the 15th, having received no answer, the army advanced down the Maumee, and on the 18th, having marched forty-one miles from Ft. Defiance, the soldiers began erecting a light fortification for the baggage, in preparation for active work. On the morning of the 20th they advanced about five miles, when they came to a place known as the Fallen Timbers—a thick wood in which the ground was covered with old trunks of trees, probably blown down by a tornado, which prevented the action of cavalry. Here the Indians were lying in ambush, to give battle.

The advance guard was received with so severe a fire that it was forced to fall back, although under orders, in case of attack, to hold its position until the army could come to its support. But there was no other confusion.

Wayne at once dispatched his cavalry on both flanks to gain the enemy's rear, and ordered his infantry, who were marching with loaded guns and fixed bayonets, to advance, raise the Indians with the bayonet, fire at short range, and chase them out of the woods without stopping. The movement was carried out to the letter. In the course of an hour the Indians were driven over two miles, and, being refused admission to Ft. Miami—the British post—they dispersed in all directions, the cavalry not having had time to reach their position.

The pursuit was carried almost under the walls of Fort Miami, whose commander sent a protest to Wayne against this "insult to the British flag." Wayne replied with a demand for the garrison's removal from United States territory, to which the com-

mander declined to accede. But he offered
no interference to the army, which remained
there for three days, destroying the crops
and property of the Indians and the storehouses of Colonel McKee, which were within
pistol shot of the fort.

The loss of the Americans was compara-
tively small, being five officers and twenty-
eight men killed, and sixteen officers and
eighty-four men wounded. Of the wounded eleven died. The loss to the Indians was
never definitely learned, but it was much
larger than that of the whites.

On the 24th the army started on its return to Ft. Defiance, laying waste the corn-
fields and villages for fifty miles on each
side of the river. Wayne reported that the
margins of the Maumee and Auglaize were
like "one continued village" for miles, and
that he never "before beheld such immense
fields of corn in any part of America, from
Canada to Florida." The work of destruction was continued at Ft. Defiance, and the
fort was strengthened for permanent occupancy.

On September 14 the army marched to
Kē-ki-oon'-gi and began building the fort op-

posite the Indian town, which was named Ft.
Wayne by Colonel Hamtramck, who was
left in command. The Indian dominion of
"the Glorious Gate of the Wabash" was ended forever, and it is fitting that the name of
the man who ended it should remain as a
permanent memorial. But the old memories
linger also, and to this day the older Miamis
call the place Kē-ki-oon'-gi.

The spirit of the Indians was broken.
They suffered much during the winter,
though the British furnished them extensive
supplies. The British governor Simcoe, aided by Colonel McKee and the Mohawk chief,
Captain Brant, tried to unite them for further resistance, but in vain. The action of
the British in refusing admission even to
wounded Indians at Ft. Miami and permit-
ting Wayne's men to destroy goods of both
Indians and British under the guns of the
fort, had convinced them that the British
were afraid of the Americans.

Wayne had been a revelation to them. The
Miamis named him The Wind (ă-lŏm'-
sĕng), on account of the way he had swept
them from the Fallen Timbers; but the Delawares named him The Blacksnake (Sūk-

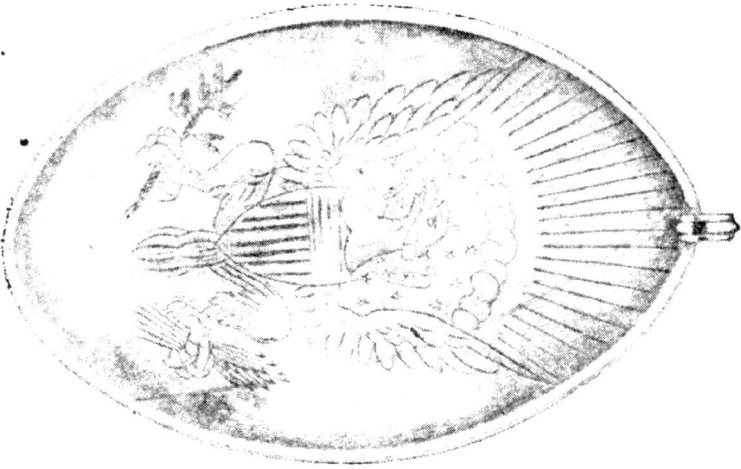

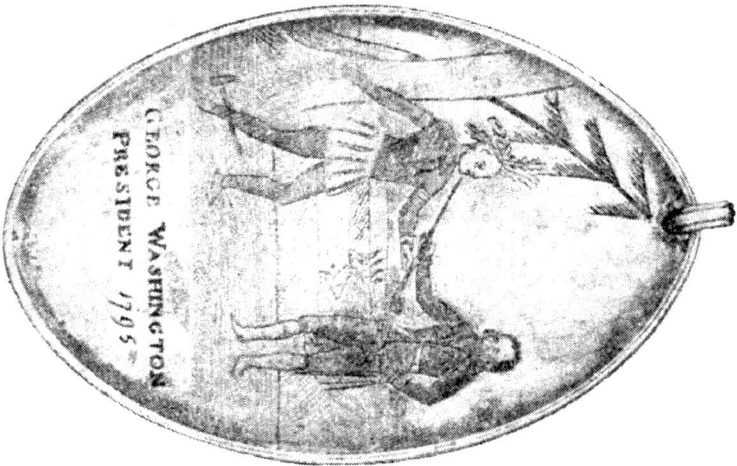

GRENVILLE TREATY MEDAL.

GEORGE WASHINGTON
PRESIDENT 1795

ach'-gook), because they esteem the blacksnake the wisest and most cunning of animals, and the most destructive to smaller animals and birds. With very little resistance the Indians obeyed his summons to assemble at Ft. Greenville in the summer of 1795, and on August 3 a treaty, which he dictated, was concluded.

The Little Turtle now realized, as few others did, that a new era had come to his people, which called for a change in them. In the past he had contended against the vices of barbarism, and had been the chief agent in suppressing "the ancient sacrificial rites," including cannibalism, which had been practiced among the Miamis as late as the Revolutionary war.

He now entered on a campaign against the vices of civilization, and an effort to gain its advantages. Most destructive of the former was intemperance. He visited the Legislatures of Ohio and Kentucky, as well as Congress, and begged for the prohibition of the liquor traffic among the Indians. In a speech, which was taken down in shorthand at the time, he denounced it as "an evil that has had so much ruin in it, that has destroyed so many of our lives, that it causes our young men to say, 'We had better be at war with the white people. This liquor that they introduce into our country is more to be feared than the gun or the tomahawk; there are more of us dead since the treaty of Greenville than we lost by the years of war before, and it is all owing to the introduction of this liquor among us.' "

While on a visit to Washington The Little Turtle learned of the benefits of inoculation as a preventive of smallpox. He at once had himself and the members of his party inoculated, and he also carried this remedy to his people, which was the means of saving the lives of many of them and of the surrounding tribes.

He tried to introduce a civilized system of agriculture among the Miamis, and at his request the Society of Friends of Baltimore, established a training farm on the Wabash. It was located at a place known as "The Boatyard," because General Wilkinson built a fleet of boats there to transport his baggage down the river. This is some two miles below the present city of Huntington, the site of which was known to the Mi-

amis as Wē'-pē-chah'-ki-oong or "The Place
of Flints," because there is here a flint ridge
running across the limestone, from which
they obtained abundant supplies of flints.

The farm was not a success, however, and
Philip Denis, the hard-headed Quaker, who
was put in charge of it, abandoned it at the
end of the first season because his Indian
pupils gave no co-operation beyond sitting
on the fence and watching him work.

The Little Turtle also endeavored to promote friendship with the Americans, and opposed British influences, which brought him
into opposition to Tecumtha. This opposition was much aggravated by his supporting
the treaties made by Governor Harrison for
lands in the southern part of Indiana. As
the Government had built a substantial log-
house for him at his town on Eel River and
otherwise encouraged him in his efforts for
civilization, his enemies found many listen-
ers to their insinuations that he had sold
himself to the Americans. This feeling was
worked up to such a point that in 1810 John
Johnston, the Indian agent, wrote to Governor Harrison: "This Turtle is contempti-
ble beyond description in the eyes of the In-

dians." Nevertheless he still retained his influence with most of the Miamis, and very few of them took part in the battle of Tippecanoe. After that event, his wisdom was again generally recognized, and he regained much of his former standing.

In his later years the old chief was much troubled by rheumatism and gout, and was treated for them by the army surgeons at Ft. Wayne. One day an interpreter rallied him with a suggestion that gout was supposed to be a disease of fine gentlemen. The Little Turtle quickly replied: "I have always thought that I was a gentleman."

And he was. He had not only a philosophic mind and a ready wit, but also a notable instinct for the proprieties that fitted him for any social surroundings. These qualities attracted attention among the whites wherever he went. One who met him while on a trip East in 1807, writes:

"The Little Turtle and Rusheville, the Beaver and Crow (Delawares), and the two Shawnees, were dressed in a costume usually worn by our own citizens of the time—coats of blue cloth, gilt buttons, pantaloons of the same color, and buff waistcoats; but they all wore leggings, moccasins and large gold rings in their ears. The Little Turtle exceeded all his brother chiefs in dignity of appearance—a dignity which resulted from the character of his mind. He was of medium stature, with a complexion of the palest copper shade, and did not wear paint. His hair was a full suit, and without any admixture of gray, although from what he said of his age, at Ft. Wayne in 1804, being then fifty-three, he must at this time have been fifty-seven years old. His dress was completed by a long red military sash around the waist, and his hat (a chapeau bras) was ornamented by a red feather. Immediately on entering the house, he took off his hat and carried it under his arm during the rest of the visit. His appearance and manners, which were graceful and agreeable in an uncommon degree, were admired by all who made his acquaintance.

The "Rusheville" here mentioned was The Little Turtle's nephew, Jean Baptiste Richardville, who succeeded him as head chief of the Miamis. His Indian name was Pi^n-jē'-wah, or the Wild Cat. He was the son of The Little Turtle's sister, Tah-kŭm-wah

(On the Other Side, i. e., in position, as across a river), and a scion of the noble French house of Drouet de Richardville. This corruption of his name is quite common, and a further twist is found in the name of Russiaville, Howard County, which was originallly intended to perpetuate his memory.

We have also attempted to commemorate a grandson of The Little Turtle in the name of the town of Coesse, in Whitley County, But this is our reproduction of his Potawatomi nickname, Kŭ-wă'-zē, or as the Miamis pronounce it, Kō-wă-zi, meaning "old," or as here "old man." He was the son of The Little Turtle's son, Mă-kŏt'-tă-mŏn'-gwah (Black Loon). His cousin, Kil-sō-kwă, says his real name was M'tĕk'-yah, meaning "forest" or "woods"; but the nickname supplanted the true name, and in the treaties he appears as "Co-i-sa," "Ko-es-say," or "Ko-was-see."

Kil-sō-kwă is the daughter of The Little Turtle's son Wŏk-shin'-gah (the Crescent Moon—literally "lying crooked"). Her mother's name was Nah-wă'-kah-mo'-kwă (the First Snow Woman—literally, the one

KILSOKWA—THE SETTING SUN.
(Granddaughter of The Little Turtle.)

that comes first). She says that her own name means "the setting sun," though literally it appears to mean only "the sun" (feminine) or "sun woman." Kil-sō-kwă married Antoine Revarre, a French-Canadian, and now lives near Roanoke, Ind., with her son Antony Revarre, whose Indian name is Wah'-pi-mŏn'-gwah (White Loon), at the advanced age of ninety-seven years.

The Little Turtle prepared to take the side of the Americans in the war of 1812, but he was destined not to participate in that conflict. His old enemy, the gout, carried him off on July 14, 1812, while at Ft. Wayne for treatment. He was buried on the bank of the St. Joseph, above Ft. Wayne, with military honors. For a generation or more the Indians were accustomed to visit his grave and pay tribute to his memory, and well they might, for if ever man served his generation to the best of his ability, this man had done so.

CHAPTER III.

THE DEATH OF THE WITCHES.

It was at the close of May, 1801, that the Moravian missionaries came to Wah'-pi-kah-mē'-kŭnk, standing where the city of Muncie now is, or rather on the bluffs across the river from Muncie. This was the easternmost of the Delaware towns on White River, and that was the cause of its name, for the trails from the east and north and south all struck it first, and so it was by pre-eminence the White River Town. This is what the name means, for in the early times the Delawares adopted the Miami name of the river, Wah'-pi-kah-mē'-ki (White Waters—varied to O'-pēē-kō-mē'-kah in the Unami dialect) though in later times they commonly called it Wah'-pi-hă'-ni, which in their own language means literally White River.

The missionaries were Brother John P. Kluge and his wife, and Abraham Luckenbach, a young man of twenty-four years, all

of whom had been called to the work from
Pennsylvania, and had passed the preceding
winter with Zeisberger at Goshen, on the
Muskingum, learning the Delaware language. They had reached this point from
Goshen after a wearisome journey of nine
weeks, partly by water down the Ohio, then
up the Miami and Whitewater, and across
through the woods. They were accompanied
by two Delaware converts, one named
Thomas, and the other an old man named
Joshua, who had formerly lived at the mission at Wyalusing (Place of the Aged Warrior—the same name was afterward given
to a stream in southern Indiana).

They were hospitably received, but the
Indians, who were pagans, pointed out a
place for them to settle some twenty miles
farther down the river. The truth is that
the pagans regarded the Christian Indians
as a sort of inoffensive idiots, who did not
have sense enough to protect themselves—
the Moravians being non-combatants—and
who might be murdered by whites, as their
brethren had been at Salem and Gnadenhuet-
ten on the Muskingum, if they did not have

a surrounding cordon of Indians of more
warlike character.

This location was favorably situated for
their labors, being only two miles east of
the large town of the chief known to the
whites as Anderson. His Indian name was
Kŏk-tō'-whă-nŭnd, which may be translated
Making a Cracking Noise, i. e., as of a house
or a tree about to fall, for that is the meaning of Kŏk-to'whă, and the ending nund indicates that the noise is caused by some person.

The whites have given the name of Anderson to the place, but the Indians did not call
it by the chief's name, as they did many
other places, but gave it the special name of
Wah'-pi-mins'-kink, or Chestnut Tree Place.
Some botanists have doubted that the chestnut tree is native to Indiana, but the earliest
surveyor's notes show that they were common in some regions. The section center
one and a half miles east of Anderson was
marked by "a chestnut thirty inches in dia-
meter."

Indeed, the location was about the only
encouraging feature of the case, for these
pagan Delawares had an ancient religion of

their own to which they were much attached. It was (and is, for it still continues)
founded on the vision of a boy who was ill-
treated at home and wandered off one night
heartsore and very hungry, until, almost exhausted, he began moaning and supplicating
the Great Spirit. As he cried out "O-oo"
he heard twelve voices repeat the sound, one
after another. Then he fell asleep and a
manitou appeared to him as a man, with one
side of his face painted red and the other
black. He told the boy all about the spirit
world, and that the troubles of his people
were due to their wickedness and their failure to worship the manitous for their good-
ness.

In answer to an inquiry about the twelve
voices he said these were the voices of the
manitous ruling in the twelve spheres of
heaven, through which one must pass to
reach the Great Spirit; and all prayers are
thus passed in by them, from one to another,
until the twelfth delivers them to the Great
Spirit.

He gave the boy full instructions for the
religious rites the Indians must observe, especially the annual thanksgiving feast, and

also for the temples or council-houses they must erect for worship. These were to be long and large, and to be divided into twelve parts, in each of which must be a post with a face carved on it, and painted red on one side and black on the other, representing the twelve ruling manitous. In the center there must be a post with four faces carved on the four sides, representing the Great Spirit who sees and knows all things.

To these houses the people must enter by the east door and retire in the same way, always passing to the right, and never going between the center post and the east door. After entering, the Turtle clan or Unami (People Down the River), commonly known among themselves by their totem name, Pa-ko-an-go (The Crawler), were to be seated on the south side. On the west are the Turkey clan, or Unalachtigo (People Near the Ocean), commonly known among themselves as Chi-ke-la-ki (from chik-e-no, a turkey), or sometimes by their other name of the turkey, Pullaeu (It Does Not Chew—referring to the bird's manner of eating). On the north are the Wolf clan, known to us as Monseys or Munsees, but properly Minsi or

Minthu (People of the Stony Country), whose totemic name is p'tuk-sit, or round foot, because they did not make a picture of a wolf for their totem, but only of its foot.

Of these houses on White River Luckenbach says: "In each of these towns there was a council-house, about forty feet in length and twenty feet in breadth, where they usually celebrated their sacrificial feasts and dances. These houses were built of split wood, piled up betwixt posts set in the ground, covered with a roof made of laths and the bark of trees, and having an entrance at either end; but there was neither floor nor ceiling; three fireplaces stood in a straight line from end to end, with large kettles suspended over them in which a mess of Indian corn and meat, boiled together, was prepared for the guests to eat, after the dance was over. Platforms one foot high and five feet wide were raised all along the sides of the house, which were covered first with bark and then long grass on top of that, to serve as couches for the guests to sit or recline upon while smoking their pipes and witnessing the dancing of the rest. These dances were invariably got up in the

night, and sometimes continued for weeks
together. The whole was concluded by a
sacrificial feast, for which the men had to
furnish the venison and bear's meat, and the
women the cornbread; and everything had
to be prepared in the council-house before all
feasted together amidst the observance of
certain rites."

And the superstitions of these pagans
were very real to them. They regarded
dreams and visions as supernatural visita-
tions quite as fully as Pharaoh did. They
believed absolutely and fearfully in witches,
which is not very surprising when one con-
siders that Blackstone had defended the English laws against witchcraft less than fifty
years earlier. They were perversely argu-
mentative, conceding that the whites had
acted very wickedly in crucifying the Savior
when he came to them, but urging that they
had never treated the manitous thus, and
that they did not see how they were con-
cerned in the offense of the whites.

But, with all their failings, they at least
preached fairly well, for Luckenbach says:
"On such occasions the chiefs usually address speeches to their people of both sexes,

DELAWARE COUNCIL HOUSE.

(As pictured by Richard C. Adams, a Delaware, representing the tribe at Washington.)

and rigidly enforce abstinence from all gross sins, especially drunkenness (although they themselves are very far from practicing what they teach), while recommending them to practice hospitality, love and concord, as things that are well pleasing to God. This proves that even savages are capable of distinguishing between good and evil, and are, therefore, possessed of a conscience that either accuses or else excuses them, and that will judge them at the last day."

Obviously the missionaries had a hard task before them, but at least they were promised an open field. Luckenbach says that soon after their coming they "were visited and welcomed by the two oldest Delaware chiefs, Packantschilas and Tetepachsit," and, although both were pagans, "both of these chiefs assured us they had given their people permission to visit us and to hear the Word of God, and that they would order them not to molest us in any way, nor to pass through our place when they were drunk." These were gratifying assurances, for the former, known to the whites as Buckongehelas, was the head war chief of the nation, and Ta-ta-pach-sit, sometimes men-

tioned as "The Grand Glaize King," was
the head chief in time of peace. His name
is given in an old Pennsylvania treaty as
"Tatabaugsuy, the Twisting Vine," but
there is nothing in it like the Delaware words
for "twisting" or "vine." Ta-ta is a Delaware double negative, making it emphatic,
and the verb pachan (pŏch-ŏn) means to divide, separate, sunder; making the literal
meaning, "It can not be divided or pulled
apart." Such a name would not be applied
to any fragile vine, and the one woody twisting vine in the old Delaware country was
the American Woodbine, of which this is presumably the specific name.

Encouraged by the assurances of these
chiefs, the missionaries proceeded with the
erection of a permanent dwelling. They
lived in hastily-constructed bark huts during the summer, but by November they completed a substantial log cabin sixteen feet
square, which gave them comfortable shelter for the winter.

The work of conversion did not proceed
with much success, and it was not long until they discovered that they were contending
against an influence even more adverse than

the ancient Delaware religion. It was a
spirit of opposition to the whites in all
things, that arose chiefly from the land question—the continual demand of the white man
for more land. Only half a dozen years had
passed since the treaty of Greenville, when
the boundaries between American and Indian were "fixed for all time," as the Indians
understood, but immediately after the treaty
there was a great flood of immigration to the
new lands, and soon there was talk of more
land being needed.

Some of the Indians promptly opposed
this, and among them none was more prominent than the young Shawnee Tecumtha. A
born orator, with eloquence as great as that
of any man his race has produced, and absolutely fearless, he proclaimed everywhere
the doctrine that the Indians were one people, that the land was their common inherit-
ance and that no tribe could give any part
of it away without the consent of all.

This doctrine was soon widely adopted,
for in 1802 General Harrison wrote that he
did not believe that he could obtain land cessions without a general assembly of the
chiefs, for: "There appears to be an agree-

ment amongst them that no proposition which relates to their lands can be acceded to without the consent of all the tribes, and they are extremely watchful and jealous of each other lest some advantage should be obtained in which they do not all participate."

Nevertheless he proceeded to treat with individual tribes. From September, 1802, to December, 1805, he negotiated seven treaties with "chiefs and head men," by which were ceded about 46,000 square miles of territory in southern Indiana and Illinois. No tribes were represented but those asserting ancient proprietary rights, although the Wyandots and Shawnees had been assured a part in the Indian lands at the treaty of Greenville. Tecumtha and his coadjutors denounced these treaties, and the chiefs who made them, and factions in all the tribes joined with them.

At some time prior to 1805 a number of Shawnees, including Tecumtha and his brother Law-le-was-i-kaw (The Loud Voice) came to live with the Delawares on White River, and it was here that Law-le-was-i-kaw took the name of Tems-kwah-ta-wah (He Who Keeps the Door Open) and

assumed the role of a prophet. He was readily accepted in this function, and under his
teaching the tribes were soon stirred to the
work of purification, which consisted chiefly
of abandoning the clothing and costumes of
the whites and driving out witchcraft. It
was notable that those accused of the latter
were chiefs who had signed the treaties or
persons who were known as friendly to the
whites. The Indians were taught that the
Great Spirit had made them a different race
from the whites, and that they must keep
themselves distinct. The tendency of the
new religion was to create hostility to the
white man in all lines.

In the spring of 1806 the situation became
so unpleasant that the missionaries decided
to remove. Pŏch-gŏnt'-shē-hē'-lŏs had died
in 1804, and Ta-ta-pach-sit was in disfavor
on account of friendship to the whites. They
were occasionally visited by drunken youths
who shot and carried off their hogs, and
showed hostility in other ways. Early in
March Luckenbach and Joshua made a trip
to the Mississinewa towns to look for a more
favorable location.

As they passed through Wah-pi-kah-me-

kunk they found the Delawares assembled
in large numbers holding council as to how
they should rid the tribe of witches. Following the plan of Tecumtha, the young men—
the warriors—had taken the reins of government into their own hands; and, following
the teaching of The Prophet, they had determined to remove all witches. If those who
were accused of witchcraft would confess
and abandon their practices they would be
forgiven, but if not they would be turned
over to "Their Grandfather, the Fire."

Immediately after the return of Luckenbach and Joshua, seven Indians painted
black appeared at the cabin of the missionaries and announced that they had come to
take Joshua before the tribunal. Old Ta-ta-
pach-sit had been arraigned for witchcraft
and had confessed, on promise of forgive-
ness if he would surrender his witch bag—
the sack in which Indian medicine men pro-
fess to carry the media of their magic. He
had declared that in the previous winter he
had given his witch bag to Joshua, who must
now confront him. Joshua went with them,
calm and unterrified in his consciousness of
innocence.

The statement as to Ta-ta-pach-sit was true. The old chief had probably given way under the weakness of old age and had hopelessly involved himself and others. It was simple enough, though weak, to admit the practice of witchcraft, of which he was entirely innocent; but when it came to surrendering or accounting for a witch-bag that he never possessed, he was lost. He had said it was hidden at various places, but search did not reveal it. He then confessed giving it to his wife, to his nephew and to Joshua, but these all denied it convincingly, and the old chief promptly brought forward some new story.

The old Munsee woman who had been serving as judge in such matters declined to decide these cases. Aside from the difficulties involved, she had had a wonderful vision in which she had devoured a light that appeared to her three times, and she construed this to be a divine reflection on her judicial standing. It was, therefore, decided to hold the accused until The Prophet, who was expected the next day, should come and decide as to their guilt in person.

On the next day, March 17, the mission-

SITE OF THE MORAVIAN MISSION ON WHITE RIVER.

aries were startled by a party of black-paint-
ed Indians who came to their place with Ta-
ta-pach-sit in custody. Hastily taking a fire-
brand from one of the Indian lodges, they
passed on to a tree, under which the old man
had now indicated the place where the witch-
bag was concealed. They dug at the place
he pointed out, but found nothing. With
gathering fury they built a fire and threatened him with instant death if he did not give
up his poison.

The frenzied dotard pointed out one place
after another and they dug in vain. It was
hopeless. He was self-convicted. His own
son struck him down with his tomahawk.
They stripped him and cast his body into the
flames. After finishing their work they
came to the cabin of the missionaries, and
the son, displaying his father's belt of wam-
pum, said: "This belonged to him who dis-
carded my mother and his oldest children
and took him a young wife."

But what of Joshua? The missionaries
were beginning to feel alarmed about him,
and ventured some words in his defense. To
this the ominous reply of the Indians was
that they ought not to speak in his behalf,

because he was a bad man who had doubtless brought many persons to death by his
magic powers. When the Indians had gone
their fears increased as they discussed the
situation, and in the morning Luckenbach
started to Wah-pi-kah-me-kunk to do what
he could for the aid or comfort of their
friend. About half way there he met the
chief Kok-to-wha-nund, who informed him
that Joshua had been killed at Wah-pi-kah-
me-kunk on the preceding day. The missionary was overcome by grief, and lament-
ed that they had slain an innocent man; but
the chief sternly answered that he deserved
his doom, and that other wicked people who
made way with their fellow-men by poison
or magic would meet the same fate.

To a protest against the barbarity of such
executions, he replied: "You white people
likewise try your criminals, and whenever
you find them guilty you hang them or exe-
cute them in some other way, and we are
now doing the same among us. Another of
our chiefs, Hackin-pom-ska, is now under
arrest on a similar charge, but his fate still
remains undecided."

There had indeed been exciting times at

Wah-pi-kah-mē'-kunk on that St. Patrick's day. The Prophet had returned and had confronted Joshua in the council-house. Joshua protested his innocence. Unable to furnish any proof against him, The Prophet declared that while it was true that he did not have the witch-bag of Ta-ta-pach-sit, he had magic powers of his own by which he was able to destroy a man's life when he wished to offer a victim to his god. This was equivalent to a judgment of guilty. The Indians conducted Joshua to a large fire which they had built. They formed a ring about him and demanded that he confess how many men he had destroyed by his magic. Joshua calmly and solemnly avowed his complete innocence.

There was a momentary halt. An Indian stepped from the circle, went to the fire, and lighted the tobacco in his tomahawk-pipe. As he passed behind Joshua he suddenly sank the tomahawk in his brain. With wild yells the others then sprang forward and rained blows on the senseless body. Then they stripped his body and threw it in the flames, where it burned to ashes.

There remained three others under accusation. The nephew of Ta-ta-pach-sit was a Christian Indian, commonly known as Billy Patterson, who had lived among the whites until he acquired considerable skill as a gun-smith. He was a strong and courageous man, with a queer mixture of religious faith and Indian stoicism and he received The Prophet's condemnation with composure. They offered him pardon if he would confess, and abandon his magic practices, but he answered with scorn: "You have intimidated one poor old man, but you can not frighten me; go on, and you shall see how a Christian and a warrior can die." He was at once burned at the stake. Bible in hand, praying, chanting hymns, and defying all the powers of evil until his voice was stifled, his brave soul passed out as from one of the martyrs of apostolic times.

The failure to elicit any confession or evidences of guilt from him was somewhat disquieting. When the council had resumed its session and was considering the case of Ta-ta-pach-sit's wife her brother entered the council-house, went forward, took her by the hand and led her out of the house. He then returned and declared in a loud voice: "The evil spirit has come among us and we are killing each other." No further attempt was made to try the woman, and the case of Hack-ink-pŏm'-ska (He Walks on the Ground) was taken up.

This chief was of different stuff from the others. He did not wait for any additional accusation. Advancing to The Prophet, he denounced him as a liar and an impostor, and threatened him with personal vengeance if he made any charge of witchcraft against him. This was a very practical test of divine protection, from the Indian point of view, to which The Prophet was not prepared to submit, and after some discussion Hack-ink-pom-ska was remanded to custody to await further proceedings, but without being deprived of his standing and authority as a chief. No further action was taken against him.

The news of these tragedies was slow in reaching Governor Harrison at Vincennes—up the trail to Ft. Wayne by runner, and down the Wabash by boat—reaching him in April. He at once sent a strong letter to the Delawares, in which he said: "Who is this pretended prophet who dares to speak

in the name of the Great Creator? Examine
him. Is he more wise or more virtuous than
you are yourselves, that he should be selected
to convey to you the orders of your God? Demand of him some proofs at least of his being the messenger of the Deity. If God has
really employed him, He has doubtless authorized him to perform some miracles, that
he may be known and received as a prophet.
If he is really a prophet, ask of him to cause
the sun to stand still—the moon to alter its
course—the rivers to cease to flow—or the
dead to rise from their graves. If he does
these things, you may then believe that he
has been sent from God." This reached the
Indians after they had ended their crusade
against witchcraft, but it probably served to
lessen somewhat the influence of The
Prophet, for in the succeeding troubles the
Delawares were generally loyal to the Americans.

And the missionaries? After learning the
situation at Wah-pi-kah-me-kunk, Luckenbach decided to go at once before the council,
which was still in session, and ask what was
the sentiment as to them. He entered the
council-house, announced that he had heard

rumors that the Indians meant to drive the missionaries away, and asked them to express their minds freely concerning their future stay.

The head men replied that the rumors had not originated with them, but possibly with some of the young men; that they had no especial preference in the matter, and had not, in fact, called for any white teachers, but had merely requested that some of their relatives at the Muskingum move out to them; of these, however, not the families expected—the White Eyes and the Killbucks —but only a few others had come. The missionaries were free to come or go as they liked; no obstacles would be put in their way. The council then advised him to consult Hack-ink-pom-ska, and this chief coincided with the council in the view that their services were not particularly desirable to the Indians, especially in view of the surplus of religion furnished by The Prophet.

On consultation with Brother and Sister Kluge it was decided to ask the authorities at Bethlehem permission to leave, although this involved a wait of five or six months. A messenger was sent and they waited through the summer, frequently annoyed by drunken and quarrelsome Indians, until at last the permission for their return came. On September 16, with their little belongings, they left the White River mission and turned back to their Pennsylvania homes.

Their cabin remained standing for a number of years, but even that did not preserve their memory. A few years later, when the white settlers came and found the Indian town known as Little Munsee sprung up about the place, it was assumed that the cabin must have been built by the Indians as a fort, because it was so much more substantial than ordinary Indian structures, and so the tradition passed down.

CHAPTER IV.

No Indian's name is more inseparably linked to the history of Indiana than that of "Tecumseh," and none is more familiar to American readers, but it is remarkable how little is definitely known about this celebrated man.

As to his death, there are three conflicting accounts, each verified by the statements of alleged eye-witnesses. As to his birth, Mc-Kenney and Hall give a romantic story of his descent from the daughter of an English Governor of Georgia or South Carolina, who took a fancy to marry a Creek warrior; but the historians of those States do not mention this unusual event, and Benjamin Drake, from whom McKenney and Hall state they had their information, says that this story was concocted by the Prophet to give importance to his family.

Drake probably is right in his statement

that Tecumtha was born at the old Shawnee town of Piqua, on Mad River, Ohio; that his father was Pŭck-e-shin'-wau (something that drops), a Shawnee of the Kiscopoke clan, and that his mother was Mē-thō-ă-tăs'-kē, Shawnee of the Turtle totem. Her name signifies a turtle laying eggs in the sand.

But Drake says the name is properly "Tecumtha," and that it means "a shooting star." Other authorities say it means "a comet," "a panther leaping on its prey," and "an obstacle in the path." Frank A. Thackery, superintendent and agent at Shawnee, Okla., writes to me: "The proper pronunciation of this name is Tē-cŭm-tha, with the accent sometimes on the first syllable and sometimes on the last, depending on the way in which the word is used. The meaning of the word in the Shawnee language is 'going crossways,' and it is used in the sense of a person crossing your path for the purpose of disputing your passage."

Other Indian authorities give it as "crossing over," "going across," "flying over," any of which explains the origin of the commonly given meanings. Gatschet conjectured that these meanings might be references to the fact that Tecumtha belonged to the Măn-e-tū′-wi-mis-si-pis′-si or Spirit Panther totem. Figuratively this totem stands for a meteor or a comet.

There is little truth in the common ideas of the cause of Tecumtha's hostility. He was a warrior, but he was not like the defiant Seminole who is supposed to have said:

"I battle for the love I have
To see the white man fall."

Tecumtha was also a statesman, and his chief end in life was to prevent a wrong to his people. The cause of this originated in the treaty of Greenville. At that time General Wayne forced the assembled tribes to accept a boundary line which gave most of Ohio to the whites and threw the Ohio tribes back into Indiana. The Ohio Indians—Wyandots, Ottawas, Six Nations of Sandusky, Delawares and Shawnees—unanimously asked General Wayne to divide the land between the several tribes. They said, in a formal address, as shown by our own official records, "We wish to inform you of the impropriety of not fixing the bounds of every nation's rights; for, the manner it now lies in, would bring on disputes forever between the different tribes of Indians, and we wish to be by ourselves, that we may be acquainted how far we might extend our claims, that no one may intrude on us, nor we upon them."

But General Wayne declined to do this, and with remarkable disregard of the point of the request said: "You Indians best know your respective boundaries," and urged them: "Let no nation or nations invade, molest or disturb any other nation or nations in the hunting grounds they have heretofore been accustomed to live and hunt upon, within the boundary which shall now be agreed on."

This decision they were forced to accept, and therefore the Ohio Indians were thrown back among the more Western tribes without having any lands set off for them. They mixed largely with the Indian tribes, many of the Delawares and Shawnees making their homes in the hitherto unoccupied parts of southern Indiana, but they advanced the theory that under the new arrangement the land belonged to all the tribes in common, and this was generally accepted.

In 1802 Governor Harrison wrote: "There

appears to be an agreement amongst them that no proposition which relates to their lands can be acceded to without the consent of all the tribes."

But the only treaty in which he undertook to get this general consent was the one of June 7, 1803, and its cessions of land were very slight—four miles square at the salt springs in southeastern Illinois, and four tracts each one mile square on the roads from Vincennes to Kaskaskia and Clarksville, for the location of taverns.

In return for this the United States was to distribute 150 bushels of salt annually among all the tribes, and to give free ferriage to all of the Indians at the ferries that might be established on these roads. This treaty was signed by three Shawnees, but in no other of Harrison's treaties did any Shawnee join, or any Wyandot, or any Ohio Delaware, and apparently they were not consulted at all, although by 1806 he had negotiated five other treaties for the cession of about 46,000 square miles of land in Illinois and southern Indiana.

These treaties were made with the "chiefs and head warriors" of various tribes, and four of them had only five Indian signers each. It was these treaties that raised the wrath of Tecumtha and his sympathizers, for not only did none of the Ohio Indians consent to them, but none received any part of the compensation, although the Indiana and Illinois Indians had shared equally in the compensation at the treaty of Greenville. It was clear that the Shawnees and other Ohio Indians were being shut out entirely; and when the treaties of 1809 were made, by which 3,000,000 acres were added to the cessions, Tecumtha became defiant and said that these treaties should not be carried into effect.

It was then that Tecumtha came to Vincennes and had his dramatic interview with General Harrison. He came to Vincennes on August 12, 1810, with a retinue of 75 warriors, and for several days there were interviews and councils between him and Governor Harrison. On the 20th an open-air council was in progress before the Governor's residence. Tecumtha made a long speech in which he urged that the treaties had been made by but few people, and that they had no right to dispose of the common heritage. He threatened vengeance on the chiefs who had signed the treaties if they were not rescinded, and he charged Harrison with having incited the trouble. He said:

"It is you that are pushing them on to do mischief. You endeavor to make distinctions. You wish to prevent the Indians to do as we wish them, to unite and let them consider their lands as the common property of the whole. You take tribes aside and advise them not to come into this measure; and until our design is accomplished we do not wish to accept your invitation to go and see the President. The reason I tell you this is, you want, by your distinctions of Indian tribes, in allotting to each a particular tract of land, to make them to war with each other. You never see an Indian come and endeavor to make the white people do so. You are continually driving the red people; when, at last, you will drive them into the great lake, where they can't either stand or work." He declared that the warriors represented the will of the Indians, and that unless the treaties were rescinded he would call a great council of the tribes to deal with the treaty chiefs.

At the close of his speech Governor Harrison began to reply. He was dwelling on the uniform justice which the United States had shown in its dealings with the Indians, when Tecumtha sprang to his feet and denounced the statement as untrue, and charged that Harrison and the United States had cheated and imposed on the Indians. With defiant gesticulation he said to the interpreter, Barron, "Tell him he lies." Barron hesitated and sought to soften the expression, but Tecumtha reiterated, "No, no. Tell him he lies." But the stir interrupted the proceedings. Several of the warriors arose and stood in a threatening attitude. General Gibson, Secretary of the Territory, who understood the Shawnee language, directed Lieutenant Jennings to advance with the guard of twelve men, who had stood at a little distance. As soon as order was restored Tecumtha's words were translated, and Governor Harrison indignantly reproached him for his conduct, and ordered him to return to his camp, saying that the council fire was extinguished and he would hold no further communication

TECUMTHA.

(From the only known portrait—a pencil sketch by Pierre le Drou, a young trader at Vincennes. Probably not an exact likeness. Represents Tecumtha in his British uniform.)

with him. Abashed by this firm stand, the Indians sullenly withdrew.

With cooling time, Tecumtha realized that he had made a diplomatic blunder. In the morning Barron visited him in his camp, and found him very desirous of a further interview and an amicable settlement. Governor Harrison consented to the interview on condition that Tecumtha would apologize for his insult, and in the afternoon the council was resumed. With perfect dignity, but in a respectful manner, Tecumtha disclaimed any intention to offer insult, and explained that he had perhaps been misinformed as to the sentiments of the white people, who, he had been told, were divided in their opinion as to the treaties; but he said he knew they already had more land than they could use, "as he had sent some of his men to reconnoiter the settlements, and had found that the lands towards the Ohio were not settled at all." Governor Harrison then asked him to state explicitly whether the Kickapoos would accept their annuities under the late treaty, and whether the surveyors who might be sent to run the boundary line, under the treaty of 1809, would be interfered with. To

this Tecumtha responded that he was authorized to say that the Kickapoos would not accept their annuities; and, as to the boundaries, "I want the present boundary line to
continue. Should you cross it, I assure you
it will be productive of bad consequences."
The council was then brought to a close.

On the next day, Governor Harrison, accompanied only by Barron, visited Tecumtha's camp, where he was politely received,
and another long interview was held, but
without different result. Tecumtha restated
his position, and when Governor Harrison
assured him that his claims would never be
admitted by the President, he replied:

"Well, as the great chief is to determine
the matter, I hope the Great Spirit will put
sense enough into his head to induce him to
direct you to give up the land. It is true, he
is so far off he will not be injured by the
war. He may sit still in his town, and drink
his wine, while you and I will have to fight
it out."

This closed the conferences of 1810, but,
in June, 1811, Governor Harrison sent a
message to Tecumtha and The Prophet,
warning them of the consequences of hos-

tilities. To this Tecumtha replied, protesting that no hostilities were intended, and saying that he would come to Vincennes in hope of a peaceable adjustment of all differences. In July the Indians began to assemble about twenty miles north of Vincennes, and when Tecumtha joined them they numbered about 300, of whom one-tenth were women and children. This gathering caused apprehension, and Governor Harrison sent a message disapproving it. Tecumtha replied that he had only twenty-four men in his party, and "the rest had come of their own accord; but that everything should be settled to the satisfaction of the Governor, on his arrival at Vincennes." To be prepared for any emergency, the militia of the county, amounting to 750 men, were called out, and guards were stationed about the town.

It was charged, and generally believed by the whites, that Tecumtha contemplated treachery. At this time about the only friends the Indians had in southern Indiana were the Shakers, who had a settlement some fifteen miles north of Vincennes. They had a mission to the Shawnees in 1807, and apparently were on much the same friendly terms with the Indians as the Quakers have usually been. The Indians who accompanied Tecumtha assembled near their settlement. One of the leading Shakers made this record:

"These were trying times with us. We had use for all the wisdom and patience we possessed. These hungry creatures were about us nearly three weeks, singing and dancing to the Great Spirit. Some of the time there were upward of two hundred, all peaceable, showed no abuse to any one, would drink no whisky, and never to our knowledge took to the value of one cucumber without leave. Nor could we discover in them the least hostile symptoms, still declaring their innocence, grieved that the people would not believe them—saying to the people: 'Look, see our squaws and children. We do not go to war so. We only come here because the Governor sent for us.' But notwithstanding all this the people moved into forts and into town, bag and baggage, all around us. Oh, how often did my soul cry out within me, Lord, God! What can ail this people? Surely the prophecy of Esdras is fulfilled upon them.

'Wit has hid itself from them, and understanding withdrawn itself into its secret chamber.' "

But whether treachery was meditated or not, Tecumtha was resolute in his opposition to the treaties. It was a hopeless situation. On the one side Tecumtha contended for the same principle that we maintained in the civil war—that the Indian lands belonged to all the Indians in common and that no one tribe could dispose of any part of it without the consent of all the tribes. On the other hand, Governor Harrison held, as he stated to the next Legislature:

"Are then the extinguishments of native title, which are at once so beneficial to the Indian, the Territory and the United States, to be suspended on the account of the intrigues of a few individuals? Is one of the fairest portions of the globe to remain in a state of nature, the haunt of a few wretched savages, when it seems destined by the Creator to give support to a large population, and to be the seat of civilization, of science, and of true religion?"

But the existence of these two theories on a frontier, even without formal war, meant

trouble. There were scarcely any Indian hostilities in the Northwest from the treaty of
Greenville until 1803, but in the decade following southern Indiana was the scene of
many a bloody tragedy. Prowling bands of
warriors fell on defenseless settlers, killing
men and carrying women and children captive. And many of the whites did not hesi-
tate to kill an Indian at any favorable opportunity, without regard to his hostile or peaceable attitude.

The danger was so great and so constant
that the territorial authorities caused blockhouses to be built at various points, and
maintained companies of rangers, who pa-
trolled the established lines of travel to protect immigrants. It was Indiana's notable
period of border warfare, and when it ended
the white man's theory was triumphant—established by blood and steel.

Tecumtha did not live to see the end, but
he never gave up his cherished hope. It was
not without reason that he charged Govern-
or Harrison with trying to make war between the Indian tribes, for the Governor's
policy alienated the Indiana tribes from Tecumtha. They received the annuities and

INDIANA IN 1811.

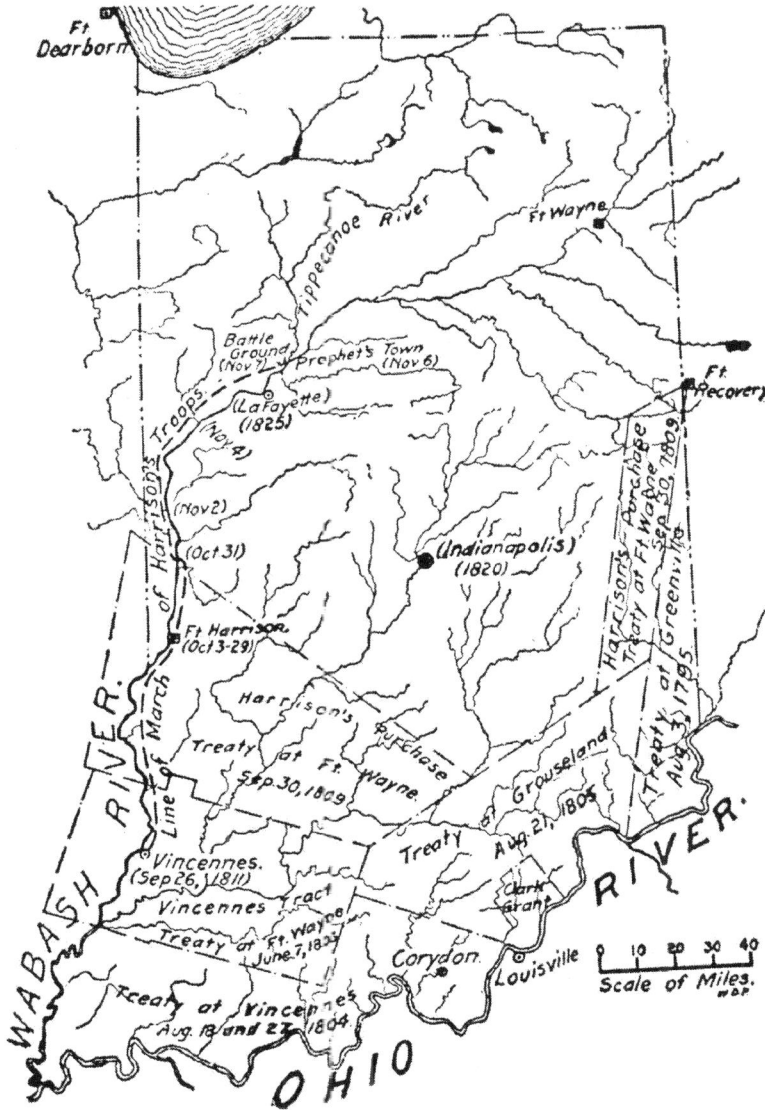

Ft. Dearborn

Tippecanoe River

Ft. Wayne

Ft. Wayne

Battle Ground (Nov 7)

Prophet's Town (Nov 6)

Ft. (Recovery)

(LaFayette) (1825)

Troops

Line of March of Harrison's

(Nov 4)

(Nov 2)

(Oct 31)

(Indianapolis) (1820)

Harrison's Purchase

Treaty of Ft. Wayne Sep. 30, 1809

Treaty at Greenville Aug. 3, 1795

Ft. Harrison. (Oct 3-29)

Harrison's Purchase

Treaty at Ft. Wayne Sep. 30, 1809

Treaty at Grouseland Aug. 21, 1805

RIVER.

Vincennes. (Sep 26, 1811)

Vincennes Tract

Treaty at Ft. Wayne June 7, 1803

Clark Grant

WABASH RIVER.

Corydon.

Louisville

Treaty at Vincennes Aug. 18 and 27, 1804

0   10   20   30   40
Scale of Miles.

OHIO

other compensation for the lands, whose sale
he opposed, and there were very few of them
in arms against the Americans, either at
Tippecanoe or in the war of 1812.

Realizing that his forces were not sufficient for successful war, disappointed repeatedly in his efforts to secure Indian allies, he hailed with joy the advent of war
with the British and enrolled with them. One
can easily imagine the chagrin with which
he saw these allies being driven back by the
Americans, and can understand the bitter-
ness of his speech to General Proctor at Malden, when the latter was preparing to retreat. His life-long dream came back as he
begged Proctor to turn the arms and ammunition over to the Indians and let them stay
and fight.

"Listen," said Tecumtha, "when war was
declared our Father stood up and gave us
the tomahawk, and told us that he was then
ready to fight and strike the Americans—
that he wanted our assistance and that we
would certainly get our land back that the
Americans had taken from us. * * * Father,
you have the arms and ammunition which
our Great Father sent for his red children.

If you have an idea of going away, give them to us. You may go, and welcome. Our lives are in the hands of the Great Spirit. We are determined to defend our land, and if it be His will, we wish to leave our bones upon it."

And undoubtedly he went into the battle of the Thames with that feeling—with the conviction that the supreme hour had come when all must be won or lost, and gave his life as the crowning sacrifice of his life's effort.

And yet this concession of Tecumtha's honesty of purpose is no reflection on Governor Harrison, but only a presentation of the different point of view. Harrison always warmly resented every charge of unfairness on his part. At the treaty of 1814, he was especially urgent that the Indians should point out any matter in which he had ever deceived them or done them injustice.

At that time Harrison said as to Tecumtha's position:

"After the treaty was made the Prophet and his brother, who had no right to participate in it, began to propagate the principle that the whole of the lands on this continent were the common property of all the tribes and that no sale could take place or would be valid unless all the tribes were parties to it. This idea is so absurd and so new, too, that it could never be admitted by the Seventeen Fires, either on their own account or on that of the tribes who live near to them and whose rights they have guaranteed; and you all know, for you were present at the discussion between Tecumseh and myself, on the subject of those lands, that this was the only claim he was able or ever attempted to set up."

Very true. Tecumtha offered a claim that was of no value under our laws, but under this construction the Ohio Indians were the only ones who ever surrendered their old homes to our Government without receiving some territory that they might call their own, elsewhere. Under it they were made absolutely homeless, except as they might be tolerated by the other tribes.

It is not strange that they did not take this view, nor that they protested against it. Looking back now, it is not hard to do them this justice. Indeed, when contemplating such a life as Tecumtha's, one may easily sympathize with the sentiment of Wendell Phillips as to the Indian:

"Neither Greece, nor Germany, nor the French, nor the Scotch, can show a prouder record. And instead of searing it over with infamy and illustrated epithets, the future will recognize it as a glorious record of a race that never melted out and never died away, but stood up manfully, man by man, foot by foot, and fought it out for the land God gave him against the world, which seemed to be poured out over him. I love the Indian, because there is something in the soil and climate that made him that is fated, in the thousand years that are coming, to mold us."

There are few Americans who have not accorded admiration to Tecumtha's manly character, but perhaps none has paid higher tribute than Charles A. Jones, the Cincinnati poet, in whose poem to "Tecumseh, the Last King of the Ohio," occur these stanzas:

Art thou a patriot?—so was he—
 His breast was Freedom's holiest
   shrine;
And as thou bendest there thy knee,
 His spirit will unite with thine;

All that a man can give, he gave—
  His life—the country of his sires
From the oppressor's grasp to save—
  In vain—quenched are his nation's
    fires.

Oh, softly fall the summer dew,
  The tears of Heaven upon his sod,
For he in life and death was true,
  Both to his country and his God;
For, oh, if God to man has given,
  From his bright home beyond the skies
One feeling that's akin to Heaven,
  'Tis his who for his country dies.

CHAPTER V.

THE FALL OF THE PROPHET.

Notwithstanding the eloquence, magnetism and high repute of Tecumtha among the Indians, there is little room for question that the chief element of strength in his confederacy was the influence of his brother, the Prophet. The original name of this man was the Loud Voice—commonly written Law-le-was-i-kaw, or Ol-la-wa-chi-ca, but more properly La-lu-e-tsee-ka. When he assumed the role of prophet, at our White River Delaware towns, in 1805, he took the name of Tĕms-kwah'-tă-wah, or He Who Keeps the Door Open. American writers have commonly denounced him as an impostor, and a conscious humbug, but there is in fact no more reason for questioning his sincerity, though he may at times have resorted to trickery to enhance his reputation, than there is for questioning the sincerity of Mahomet or Joan of Arc or our own Mrs. Eddy. Al-

most all Indians believe in the supernatural
character of visions and dreams and their
common teaching is that if a person will pur-
ify himself and fast and pray for a week or
so, the Manitous will reveal themselves to
him. A week's fasting naturally produces
visions, which are accepted as spiritual visi-
tations in answer to prayer.

Among the white contemporaries of the
Prophet, almost the only ones who credited
his sincerity were the Shakers, who are
among the few sects who accept literally
the prophecy that "your old men shall see
visions and your young men shall dream
dreams." They sent three missionaries to
the Shawnees in 1807, and one of these, Richard McNemar, records the Prophet's own
story of his divine calling as follows:

"He [the Prophet] had formerly lived on
White River; had been a doctor and a very
wicked man. About two years ago, while
attending on sick people at Attawa, in a
time of general sickness, he was struck with
a deep and awful sense of his sins; cried
mightily to the Good Spirit to show him
some way of escape, and in his great distress
fell into a vision, in which he appeared to be

IS-KWAH-TA-WAH (HE WHO KEEPS THE DOOR OPEN)
THE SHAWNEE PROPHET.

(From Portrait formerly in National Gallery.)

traveling along a road, and came to where it forked. The right-hand way, he was informed, led to happiness, and the left to misery.

"This fork in the road, he was told, represented that stage of life in which people were convicted of sin; and those who took the right-hand way quit everything that was wicked and became good. But the left-hand road was for such as would go on and be bad, after they were shown the right way. They all move slow till they come here, but when they pass the fork to the left then they go swift. On the left-hand way he saw three houses—from the first and second were pathways that led into the right-hand road, but no way leading from the third. This, said he, is eternity. He saw vast crowds going swift along the left-hand road, and great multitudes in each of the houses, under different degrees of judgment and misery. He mentioned particularly the punishment of the drunkard. One presented him a cup of liquor resembling melted lead; if he refused to drink it he would urge him, saying: 'Come, drink—you used to love whisky.' And upon drinking it his bowels were seized with an exquisite burning. This draught he had often to repeat. At the last house their torment appeared inexpressible; under which he heard them scream, cry pitiful and roar like the falls of a river.

"He was afterward taken along the right-hand way, which was all interspersed with flowers of delicious smell, and showed a house at the end of it, where was everything beautiful, sweet and pleasant; and still went on learning more and more; but in his first vision he saw nothing but the state of the wicked, from which the Great Spirit told him to go and warn his people of their danger, and call upon them to put away their sins and be good. Whereupon he began to speak to them in great distress, and would weep and tremble while addressing them. Some believed, were greatly alarmed, began to confess their sins, forsake them and set out to be good. This spread the alarm and brought many others from different tribes to see and hear, who were affected in like manner. But some of the chiefs, who were very wicked, would not believe and tried to keep the people from believing and encouraged them on in their former wicked ways. Whereupon the Great Spirit told him to separate from these wicked chiefs and their people, and showed him particularly where to come, toward the big ford where the peace was concluded with the Americans [i. e., Greenville, O.], and there make provision to receive and instruct all from the different tribes that were willing to be good. Accordingly all that believed had come and settled there, and a great many Indians had come to hear, and many more were expected. That some white people were afraid, but they were foolish, for they would not hurt any one."

The moral teachings of the Prophet were not objectionable, as the sins he specially condemned were witchcraft, lying, stealing, poisoning people, fighting, murdering, drinking whisky, beating their wives and lewdness, but he taught also that acceptance of the customs of the whites was a sin for Indians, for which they were being punished. And these have always been the general lines of the teachings of Indian prophets. They had been followed by the great Delaware prophet, forty years earlier, who was largely instrumental in bringing on the conspiracy of Pontiac (Ottawa for "an anchor pole"—i. e., a pole thrust in the bottom of a lake or river for holding a small boat). They have been followed by most of the Indian prophets since then, as may be seen in the admirable study of "The Ghost Dance Religion," by our Indiana ethnologist, James Mooney, which forms the second volume of the fourteenth annual report of the Bureau of Ethnology. It is the natural hope of a people who feel themselves being crushed by a superior power that the Almighty will in some way intervene in their behalf, if they repent and abandon their sins. But this also naturally encourages hostility to the superior race among the younger and more warlike individuals, and it certainly had that effect in this case.

In the spring of 1808 The Prophet and his followers moved from Greenville to the Wabash, just below the mouth of the Tippecanoe. Their town there is commonly called Kethtippecanunk, which should be Kē-tăp'-ē-kŏn-nūnk' for it means Tippecanoe town, or place, and the Potawatomi name of that stream is Kē-tăp'-ē-kŏn—in Miami Kē-tăp'-kwŏn, which is the name of the buffalo fish, formerly abundant in the river. This was in the territory of the Potawatomis, who always had a strong tendency to the supernatural, as is shown by the names they have left us. There is Manitou Lake, which they believed to be inhabited by an evil spirit. Near it is a tributary of the Tippecanoe, to which the people of the vicinity still give the proper Potawatomi name of Chip-wah-nŭck', or Ghost Hole, and which has some connection with the mysteries of the lake. The St. Joseph River—the principal stream of their country—they called Sahg'-wah-sē'-pē, which may be translated Mystery River, for sahg'-wah means a mushroom, or anything that comes up in the night without any seed having been planted. Their legend of the origin of this name is that they once found a strange Indian sitting on the bank of this stream, and no one ever learned who he was or whence he came; so they called him, and also the stream, Sahg'-wah.

Most curious of all is the name Shipshewana, given to a lake and its outlet stream in Lagrange County. Wah-wē-ăs'-sēē (Full Moon—literally the Round One), a grandson and namesake of the old chief for whom Lake Wawasee was named, more commonly

known as Thomas Topash—his mother, old
Wahweasee's daughter, having married a
Miami named Topash (Sweating; i. e., as a
pitcher of cold water collects moisture on a
warm day)—says this is properly Shŭp'-shē-
wah'-nō, and means "Vision of a Lion."
Whatever a Potawatomi sees in a vision after fasting is called "wah'-nō," and the original Indian of this name saw a lion. To my
remonstrance that lions were not found in
this country, and that the name must have
been given long before a Potawatomi ever
saw a lion, he replied: "That is nothing. The
Indians see everything in their visions. They
saw the whites long before they came to this
country. They have seen all the animals at
the bottom of the sea, that nobody ever saw.
This man saw a fierce, wild beast, with a big
head and mane, and afterward when the Indians saw a lion they knew it was shŭp'-shē."

At the new home on the Wabash, The
Prophet's religion prospered greatly, and its
fame spread far and wide. Hunter, the Indian captive, and others tell of its spread
among the Odjibwas and other tribes of the
North, how they abandoned whisky, discard-
ed textile clothing and returned to skins,

threw away their witch-bags, killed their
dogs and abandoned the white man's ways,
even to giving up flint and steel for making
fires and resuming the primitive and tedious
mode of rubbing two dry sticks together.
Others tell of its spread to the Osages, west
of the Mississippi, and to the Cherokees,
Creeks and other Southern tribes. Hundreds
gathered to the village, where the life was
of religious solemnity. There were public
services morning and evening, with speak-
ers who discoursed on the duties of man, the
pauses of their sermons being noted by a
loud "seguoy," or sort of "amen," from the
hearers. McNemar says of one of these
services: "On this occasion our feelings were
like Jacob's when he cried out, 'How dread-
ful is this place! Surely the Lord is in this
place!' And the world knew it not."

With the growth of the new religion the
alarm of the whites increased. Těmskwah-
tăwah protested to General Harrison that his
designs were peaceable, but depredations on
the frontier continued, and from friendly
Indians on all sides came assurances that he
meant open war as soon as he was strong
enough. Tecumtha himself openly declared

that the boundary lines of the treaty of 1809 should not be run. Finally, in 1811, Governor Harrison and the national authorities decided that the safety of the frontiers demanded the breaking up of The Prophet's town.

In September, the chief part of the forces for the expedition having been assembled, they moved up the Wabash to a point two miles above Terre Haute, where Fort Harrison was built. After completing it, and being reinforced by the rest of the troops called for, the expedition proceeded on October 28. It was composed of nine companies of regulars—eight from the Fourth Regiment and one from the Rifle Regiment; six companies of infantry from the Indiana militia, and Biggers' company of Indiana Riflemen; three companies of Indiana Mounted Riflemen; two companies of Indiana Dragoons; two companies of Kentucky Mounted Riflemen, and a company of scouts and spies. The companies were small, the entire force aggregating a little over one thousand, of whom one-fourth were mounted. On October 31, having passed Big Raccoon Creek (Hough's map marks this stream Che-que-ak

—evidently intended for Shē'-qui-ah, which is the Miami term for a poor, or lean, raccoon), the army crossed the Wabash near the present town of Montezuma. From this point it kept to the prairie country on the west side of the river, to avoid possibility of ambush. On November 2, the army camped two miles below the mouth of the Big Vermillion, and erected a blockhouse twenty-five feet square, at which a small guard was left to protect the boats that had been used in bringing the supplies thus far. The army then proceeded through the prairies, usually at some distance from the river, and on November 6 came in sight of The Prophet's town. The scouts were sent forward to ask a conference with The Prophet, but as some Indians appeared and seemed to attempt to cut them off, they were recalled, and the army moved forward. It had come to about one hundred and fifty yards from the town when some Indians came out and asked a halt and a conference. It was agreed that the troops should go into camp over night at what is now known as "the battle ground," and that hostilities should be suspended until a conference could be held on the following day. Governor Harrison says of the camping place, "It was a piece of dry oak land rising about ten feet above the level of a marshy prairie in front [i e., to the southeast], and nearly twice that height above a similar prairie in the rear, through which and near to this bank ran a small stream clothed with willows and other brushwood. Toward the left flank this bench of land widened considerably, but became gradually narrower in the opposite direction, and at the distance of one hundred and fifty yards terminated in an abrupt point." Here the troops were disposed in hollow formation, the left flanks of front and rear lines being occupied by the regulars and the right by Indiana militia. The left flank was covered by the Kentucky militia, back of whom were the dragoons, and the right flank by Spencer's Mounted Riflemen. Although no attack was anticipated, all preparations were made for it, except fortifying the camp, and Harrison said this was omitted for lack of axes. The men slept on their arms, and explicit orders were given for forming the lines in case of attack.

There has been some contention as to the

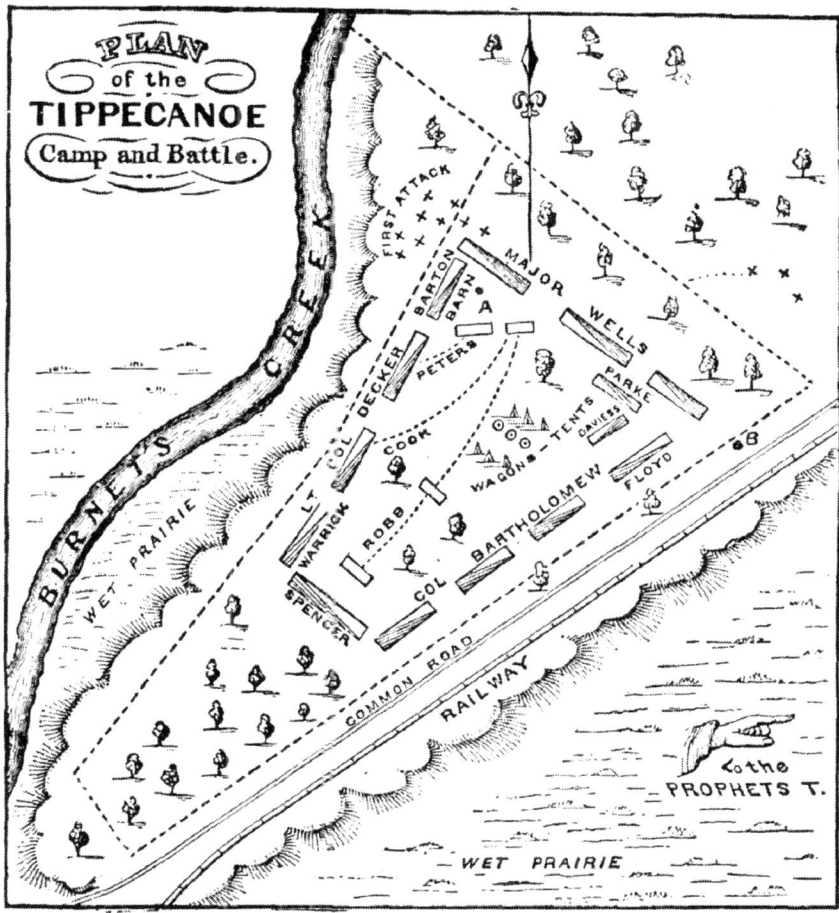

PLAN of the TIPPECANOE Camp and Battle.

intent of the Indians, and the events of that
night, but the truth was probably told later
by White Loon (Wah-pi-mŏn'-gwah), one
of the leading chiefs present. He said that
there was no intention to attack until the
Potawatomi chief Winamac (Cat Fish—literally mud fish), arrived and insisted on it.
A council was convened and most of the
chiefs opposed attack, but Winamac denounced them as cowards, said it was now
or never, and threatened unless the attack
was made to withdraw and take with him the
Potawatomis, who formed about one-third
of the town. Then the attack was agreed
to. White Loon, Winamac and Stone Eater
(Să'-nē-mă-hŏn'-ga) were put in command,
the Indian force being about equal to that
of the whites. The Prophet made a speech,
in which he assured them of success, saying
that his charms would protect them from
the bullets of the whites, and the warriors
went into the battle as confident of supernatural protection as any religious fanatics
that ever lived.

They had intended to attack on three sides
simultaneously, but a sentinel, Stephen
Mars, caught sight of them as they crept

in close to the lines, up the bank from Burnetts' Creek, at the northwest angle, and fired the alarm shot. .The Indians who were close enough attacked at once, breaking the lines at some points and in two or three instances penetrating to the tents. Mars was killed as he fled. The recklessness of the assault showed their faith in The Prophet's protection, and it took two hours of stubborn fighting to convince them of its futility.

Governor Harrison was quickly at the point of attack after the first firing, and, finding the lines at that point somewhat broken, ordered up two companies for support. By that time a heavy firing began at the northeast angle, and Harrison, turning there, found Maj. Jo Daveiss (this is the correct spelling—not Daviess, as it has been handed down) anxious to charge the enemy. After two refusals he was given permission to charge, and dashed forward with only twenty men. The Indians fell back from the front and gathered on their flanks, pouring in a heavy fire that drove back the charging party, with Major Daveiss mortally wounded. The firing now extended all around the camp, and was especially heavy on the left flank, where, as on the right flank, the Indians could approach on high ground under cover of the trees. The morning was dark and cloudy, and it had rained intermittently during the night. The campfires gave the Indians the advantage in aiming, and they were extinguished as soon as possible. The lines were reinforced wherever needed, and held intact. So the fight went on in the dark, from a little after four o'clock till daybreak, when gallant charges were made on the right and left flanks, and the Indians were chased into the marshes where the horsemen could not follow. They did not return.

The pursuit was not extended far, for the army had its hands full. Thirty-seven men had been killed, and 151 wounded, of whom twenty-five afterwards died. The cattle had escaped, and had been driven away; and the troops had recourse to horse-flesh for meat. A report was started that Tecumtha was on his way to the place with 1,000 warriors. November 7th was occupied with burying the dead, caring for the wounded, and throwing up breastworks of logs. On the 8th the mounted men advanced to the town, and found that the Indians had deserted it in

THE PROPHET'S ROCK.

haste, leaving almost all their possessions.
After gathering up the copper kettles, with
what corn and beans they could carry, the
troops applied the torch and destroyed all
that was left. There remained no doubt
that the Indians knew they were whipped.
Their force in the fight was probably about
equal to that of the whites, and although reports as to their loss varied widely, it is certain that it was no less than that of the
troops. Tecumtha was not in the vicinity,
having gone south to try to secure the alliance of the southern tribes, and it is very
well established that The Prophet had given
battle in defiance of Tecumtha's express orders.

He had met defeat, and it was more than a
mere defeat. A religion was shot and bay-
oneted to death on that field. Across Burnett's Creek stands a large boulder, known
to this day as The Prophet's Rock. Either
on this or, as some say, on a bluff farther to
the east, The Prophet stood as his men
fought, making his charms and singing his
incantations to the Manitous. But to his
appeals the bullets of the frontiersmen gave
back the mocking answer of Elijah to the

prophets of Baal—"Cry aloud," for "perad-venture he sleepeth and must be awaked." Was he sincere? Did he expect supernat-ural aid? Certainly he staked his all on the outcome. And he lost all; for even his most devoted followers realized that, if there was any divine interference at that time, the stars in their courses fought against Tenskwahta-wah.

After the battle he sought to explain the disaster by saying that his wife had touched his sacred instruments and destroyed the charm, but in vain. His reputation as a prophet was gone. For awhile he took ref-uge with a party of Wyandots on Wild Cat Creek (often called Ponce Passu, or Ponceau Pichou, corruptions of the French name Panse au Pichou, which is a literal transla-tion of the Miami name Pi^n-jē'-wah-mō'-ti, or Wildcat's Belly); but soon he retired to Canada, and later in life joined a band of Shawnees west of the Mississippi, where he died in 1834. Catlin, who met him and painted his portrait there in 1832, speaks of him as "doomed to live the rest of his days in silence, and a sort of disgrace; like all men in Indian communities who pretend to great medicine in any way, and fail; as they all think such failure an evidence of the displeasure of the Great Spirit, who always judges right."

CHAPTER VI.

WILLIAM WELLS.

One of the most trying ordeals of the pioneers, in Indian warfare, was the captivity of children. Their parents naturally imagined that they were doomed to lives of hardship and misery, but in reality they were more often adopted by Indian families, in place of lost children of their own, and treated with all the indulgence shown to their own. This was especially so with healthy, promising children, and the more so if they showed spirit.

For example, Peter Smock, grand-uncle of Wm. C. Smock, of Indianapolis, was carried off from Kentucky and adopted in the family of a Potawatomi named Winamac (Catfish). The squaws first tried to make a servant of him, but when he was left to care for a child, he pinched and otherwise maltreated it until his services as a nurse became undesirable. At this the Indians merely laughed, and said there was no use of trying to make a squaw of him; that he was a brave. They next tried to make him hoe corn, but soon found that he dug up much more than he hoed. Then the squaws tried to wash him in a stream, which is their process of "washing out the white blood and making an Indian," but he got one of them under the water and came near drowning her before she was rescued. This feat put him in still higher favor, and he was not troubled thereafter.

Among the children carried into captivity from Kentucky was William Wells. He was captured in 1774 by a band of Miamis, when about eight years old, at the home of the Hon. Nathaniel Pope. He was a sturdy, spirited lad, with high courage and an aptness for hunting that quickly made him a favorite. Heckewelder says he was adopted by a Miami named Gawiahatte, or the Hedgehog, but there must be some error in this, for Gawiahatte is Delaware, and the Miami word for hedgehog is ah'-kah-wit. The tradition handed down in the Wells family is that he was adopted by The Little Turtle. Kil-sō-kwă says that the Miamis

called William Wells A-pe-kon-it, and that
this is the name of a plant called the "wild
potato," which grows in mucky land. There
are several native plants called "wild potato"
or "Indian potato." One is the "man of the
earth" (ipomea pandurata), one of the
morning glory family, which has tubers
reaching ten pounds or more in weight. Another is the Jerusalem artichoke (helianthus
tuberosa), which the Shawnees call to-pe-ka,
but our Miamis call it o^n-zah-pă-kŏt'-tĕk, or
"yellow flower." These grow in dry soil,
and ă-pē-kŏn'-it is what we know as the
"ground-nut" or "wild bean" (apios tuberosa), which grows in low ground.

Wells grew very fully into Indian ideas.
Heckewelder, who knew him well, says he
once came upon him after he had shot a
bear, and broken its back. The bear was
whining piteously, and Wells was standing
in front of it, gravely talking to it, and occasionally striking it on the nose with his ram-
rod. Heckewelder asked him what he had
said to the bear and he replied: "I have up-
braided him for acting the part of a coward;
I told him that he knew the fortune of war;
that one or the other of us must have fallen;

that it was his fate to be conquered, and he ought to die like a man, like a hero, and not like an old woman; that if the case had been reversed, and I had fallen into the power of my enemy, I would not have disgraced my nation as he did, but would have died with firmness and courage, as becomes a true warrior."

The Indians accorded Wells the standing his merits warranted. He became a close friend of Little Turtle, who gave him his daughter in marriage, and thereafter they were constant companions. Wells served with distinction under his father-in-law in the defeats of Harmar and St. Clair, winning admiration by his dash and courage.

It is commonly stated that after the latter affair Wells seriously reflected on the fact that he was fighting his own people, and might shed the blood of his own kindred, and on this account decided to join the whites. The story handed down in the Wells family differs from this. Their version, given as coming from Wells himself, is that Wells and The Little Turtle were in entire accord in their views of the situation, and especially as to the necessity of bringing about amica-

ble relations between the Indians and the
United States. For this reason it was agreed
that Wells should join Wayne and use his
influence with the whites while The Little
Turtle tried to bring about a more pacific
frame of mind among the Indians. The two
parted at a point on the Maumee, some two
miles east of Ft. Wayne, long known as "the
Big Elm." With clasped hands, and both
men visibly affected, Wells said: "Father,
when the sun reaches the noon mark I shall
leave you and go to my people. We have always been friends and always will be
friends. Upon the field of battle we may
meet again. Let the result be what it may,
the purity of the motives prompting us, and
our common love for the wronged Indians
must be our warrant; and we may well trust
the Great Spirit for results that will vindi-
cate our action this day." Wells then made
his way to the army of General Wayne, who
made him captain of a company of spies and
he served in that capacity until after the battle of the Fallen Timbers, rendering invalu-
able service. There are two facts that go to
confirm this story. One is the known opposition of The Little Turtle to fighting

CAPT. WILLIAM WELLS.

(From a medallion portrait, now in possession of his great-great-niece, Mrs. Thos. W. McCluer, of O'Fallon, Mo.)

Wayne. The other is the fact that Wayne, after reaching the Maumee with his army, sent out messengers to the Indians urging them to come to him and make peace, although every effort in that direction theretofore had been wholly unavailing.

With the coming of peace, Wells rejoined his Indian friends at Fort Wayne. His friendship with Little Turtle was resumed, and he accompanied that great chief on his various journeys, acting as his interpreter. He learned to read and write well, and studied all the books he could obtain, being aided in this by General Harrison and others. He served as justice of the peace for a number of years, and also as Indian agent at Fort Wayne. He aided Little Turtle in keeping the Miamis out of Tecumtha's forces, and there was comparative peace after the battle of Tippecanoe through the early part of 1812. In May of 1812 a large council of Indians was held on the Mississinewa, in which were deputations of Wyandots, Chippewas, Ottawas, Potawatomies, Delawares, Miamis, Kickapoos, Shawnees and Winnebagos. They all made protestations of friendship, including Tecumtha himself.

But on June 18 the United States declared war on Great Britain, and thereafter British emissaries were actively engaged in calling the Indians to their aid. On July 17 the American post at Mackinac surrendered to a force of British and Indians. A large force menaced Detroit, where General Hull was in command, and early in August, pursuant to directions from Washington, from General Macomb, commanding the army. General Hull directed Captain Heald, commanding Fort Dearborn, to evacuate the fort, if practicable, and in that event, to distribute all the United States property contained in the fort, and in the United States factory or agency, among the Indians in the neighborhood. At the same time General Hull requested Captain Wells, then Indian agent at Fort Wayne, to proceed to Fort Dearborn with a party of friendly Miamis, to escort the garrison and the whites there to Detroit.

Fort Dearborn was at the site of Chicago. It was built in 1803, and stood on the south bank of the Chicago river near its mouth. It was a log structure, with blockhouses at northwest and southeast corners. On the

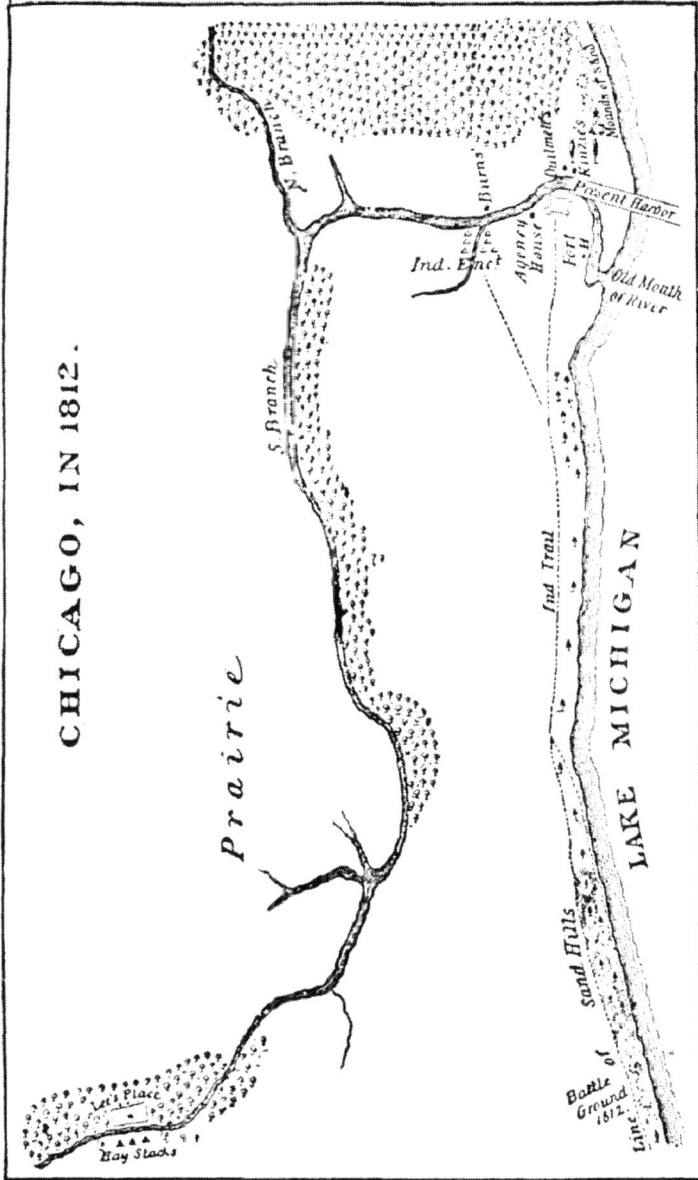

CHICAGO, IN 1812.

Prairie

N. Branch

S. Branch

Lee's Place

Hay Stacks

Burns
Ouilmett's
Kinzie's
Mound s &c.
Present Harbor
Agency House
Fort
Ind. Enc't
Old Mouth of River

Ind. Trail

LAKE MICHIGAN

sand Hills

Battle Ground 1812

Line of

north side was a subterranean passage, or
sally port, leading from the parade ground
to the river, designed for escape in emergency, and for water supply in case of siege.
The whole was surrounded with a strong
palisade of posts set on end. It was garri-
soned by fifty-four regulars and twelve militiamen under Capt. Nathan Heald. The
site was historic. When first known by the
whites, "Chicagou" was a large Miami
town. There has been much discussion as
to the meaning of the name, some affirming
that it means "the place of the skunk," and
others "the place of wild onions." The reason of this confusion is that the stem "she-
kaug" enters into both the word for skunk
and the word for onion, and in such case the
only way to get the exact meaning is from
the reason of the name. This was given by
Lamothe Cadillac in 1695, who said it was
called "the place of garlic" or wild onions,
on account of the quantity of this plant that
grew there; and this is confirmed by other
early French writers.

On August 9, in the afternoon, the Potawatomi chief, Winamac (or Winimeg—
Catfish), arrived at the fort with the orders

from General Hull for its evacuation. After
delivering them he went to John Kinzie, a
trader at the post, and urged that the post
be not abandoned; that the garrison had
ammunition and provisions for a six months'
siege; but that if Captain Heald decided to
leave the post the evacuation should be made
at once, and without notice to the Indians,
who, he said, were hostile. This was com-
municated to Captain Heald, but he said his
orders were to distribute the goods, and he
must assemble the Indians for that purpose,
if he acted conscientiously. And in justice
to Captain Heald it should be remembered
that his course was approved by his su-
periors, and that he was promoted soon
afterward.

The Indians were accordingly notified to
assemble, and it was soon observed that their
spirit was hostile. On the 12th Heald held
a council with them before the fort. The
other officers declined to attend, having
heard that the younger warriors intended
to assassinate the officers at this time; but
remained in the fort and trained the loaded
cannon on the assembly, which perhaps prevented any outbreak at the time. From the
first the minor officers and men opposed

evacuating the fort and remonstrated with Heald. He said that even if he desired to stay he lacked provisions. It was answered that there were cattle enough to keep them for six months. He urged that he had no salt to preserve the meat. It was suggested that it be "jerked," but he insisted that he must obey orders and abandon the post.

It was a trying situation. On one side the officers and men were opposed to leaving the fort, almost to the point of mutiny, and the traders and friendly Indians agreed with them; while on the other hand Heald appeared to be impelled by a conscientious sense of duty, without regard to consequences, comparable only to that which led the Modoc peace commissioners into the death-trap of the lava beds. He had told the Indians on the 12th that they would leave the fort, and divide the goods among them, and this he finally consented to modify on the urgent advice of Kinzie and others, by withholding and destroying the liquor and the surplus arms and ammunition. On the 13th another council was held with the Indians, and the surplus provisions, paints, clothes and ordinary supplies were divided among them. That night the liquor, arms and ammunition were carried into the sally-port, the liquor emptied into the river, and the arms and ammunition destroyed. But the Indians learned of this, and these were the supplies that they most desired. They afterward said that their destruction was the cause of their attack on the troops.

On the 14th Captain Wells arrived with thirty-two Miamis to aid the garrison. He, too, had prepared to oppose the evacuation, but the provisions and ammunition and arms were now gone, and it was too late to attempt to hold the fort. The Indians showed increased signs of hostility. On the evening of the 14th the Black Partridge (Ma-kah-ta-pa-ke), a friendly Potawatomie, came to the quarters of Captain Heald and said: "Father, I come to deliver up to you the medal I wear. It was given me by the Americans, and I have long worn it in token of our mutual friendship. But our young men are resolved to stain their hands with the blood of the whites. I can not restrain them, and I will not wear a token of peace while I am compelled to act as an enemy."

On the morning of the 15th, at 9 o'clock,

the garrison began its march from the fort.
Wells, with fifteen of his Miamis, were in
advance. Then came the soldiers; then the
wagons with the women and children, the
remainder of the Miamis bringing up the
rear. Some five hundred Indians marched
along with them, having promised Heald to
act as an escort. Wells had blackened his
face, as these Indians do on the warpath.

As they marched out, the musicians
played the dead march from Saul, symboliz-
ing the evacuation, and also, unconsciously,
the tragedy to follow. The Indian trail they
followed led along the lake beach. About
half a mile from the fort there began a ridge
of sand hills about a hundred yards back
from the lake. As they reached this point
the Indians left them and moved back to the
prairie behind the sand hills, and when there
hurried forward behind the hills and took
a position for attack. About a mile farther
on Wells came riding back, crying, "They
are about to attack us; form instantly and
charge on them." His words were followed
by a shower of bullets from the sand hills.
The soldiers formed in line and charged,
gaining the summit of one of the hills. They

fought gallantly, but they were only a handful surrounded by ten times their number of savages. The Miamis deserted and went over to the enemy at the outset. The soldiers continued their defense until half of their number had fallen, when the Indians made signs for a parley. Captain Heald went forward alone, and was met by Black Bird (Ma-kah-ta-pe-na-she), who promised protection to the survivors if they would surrender. Captain Heald accepted the terms and the battle ended.

During the fighting Wells turned back to the wagons, apparently apprehensive for the women and children. He came up to Mrs. Heald, who was his favorite niece, the daughter of his brother, Col. Samuel Wells. He was bleeding at the mouth and nostrils, and told her he was fatally wounded, but that he had killed seven of the redskins. He asked her to tell his wife that he had died fighting for their protection. He then turned back to the fight, but soon noticed that the Indians had gained the wagons and were tomahawking the women and children. Shouting, "Is that their game, butchering women and children? Then I will kill, too," he turned his horse toward the Indian camp, where they had left their squaws and children. He was pursued by a number of Indians, but he urged his horse on, lying flat on its neck as he loaded his gun, and turning occasionally to fire, until a ball killed his horse, and he fell under it, entangled in the stirrup. At this point Winamac and Wauban-see (The Looking Glass) ran forward to save his life, but as they got him on his feet another Indian stabbed him in the back and ended his life. The Indians cut his heart out and ate it, under their idea that in this way his courage would be transmitted to them.

In this affair twenty-six regulars, twelve militiamen, two women and twelve children were killed. The Kinzies, with Mrs. Heald, Mrs. Helm and Sergeant Griffith were saved through the good offices of Black Partridge, Sau-gan-ash (Englishman, commonly known as Billy Caldwell), To-pen-i-bee (Quiet Sitting Bear—the head chief of the Potawatomis—the name appertains to the bear totem) and other friendly Indians. Captain Heald and Lieutenant Helm, both of whom were wounded, were also saved by friendly

FORT DEARBORN MONUMENT.
(Black Partridge saving the life of Mrs. Helm.)

Indians. Most of the wounded were killed
and the remaining prisoners were dispersed
among the Indians during the winter. Part
of them were sent to Detroit to be ransomed
in the spring. Six are known to have been
killed or to have died of exposure in captivity. Mrs. Burns and Mrs. Lee, with their
infant children, were surrendered later by
the Indians, as was also the wife of Sergeant
Holt.

The fighting and the massacre occurred
practically in the space now bounded by
Michigan and Indiana avenues and Fourteenth and Twenty-first streets, in the city
of Chicago. The sand hills were long ago
removed. Having plundered the fort, on
the morning after the massacre, the Indians
set fire to it and destroyed it. So ended the
first Fort Dearborn. In 1816 the fort was
rebuilt and the bones of the victims of the
massacre, which had lain where they fell,
were then gathered up and buried near the
foot of Madison street. Later, owing to the
washing of the river and the lake, they were
reinterred by the authorities of Chicago.

CHAPTER VII.

THE DEFENSE OF FORT HARRISON.

When General Harrison marched up the Wabash to Tippecanoe, in 1811, Capt. Spier Spencer's company of mounted riflemen, from Harrison County, familiarly known as "the Yellow Jackets," started behind the main force. They were a gorgeous body, wearing yellow jackets and yellow shirts with red fringe, and with black-tipped red plumes in their hats. According to the journal of John Tipton, who was one of them, they had a very sociable and pleasant time on the march, and on October 3 Tipton, who was one of the most original and artistic of spellers that Indiana ever produced, made this entry:

"Thursday 3d marched at 9 four of our horses missing three men left to hunt them marchd one mile came to tare holt an oald indian village on the East side of Wabash on high land near a Large Prairie Peach

and aple trees growing the huts torn down
by the armey that campd here on the 2d
two miles further came up with the armey.
horses found. Campd on the river on beau-
tifull high ground to build a garison."

This was the beginning of Fort Harrison.
The "oald indian village" stood where the
city of Terre Haute now stands, and was
commonly called by the same name, as Tipton indicates, but it was also sometimes
called "Old Orchard Town," and sometimes
"The Lower Wea Town," or "We-au-ta-
non." It was a village of We-ah-ta-nons,
who were a tribe of the Miamis. The name
Terre Haute was applied to the locality before the village existed, or as the English
put it, "The Beginning of the Highlands,"
for here the bottom lands of the Wabash
begin to narrow, as you go upstream, and
this point marked the dividing line on the
Wabash between the French provinces of
Canada and Louisiana.

Fort Harrison, while primarily a relay
point for the Tippecanoe expedition, was designed as a permanent defense for Vincennes and the frontiers. On Sunday, October 27, Tipton notes "the garrison christ-

ened and extra whisky issued;" and on Tuesday the army moved on. The fort was the ordinary log structure of the time, with blockhouses at two opposite corners, from whose projecting upper stories the outside of the inclosing pickets could be reached by the guns of the garrison. After the Tippecanoe campaign it was occupied by a company of the Seventh Regiment of United States regulars, under Capt. Zachary Taylor, afterward President of the United States; and in the fall of 1812, as was usual at frontier posts, a number of the soldiers were incapacitated or debilitated by ague and malarial fever. There had also been several desertions.

On the 3d of September some friendly Miamis informed Captain Taylor that the Indians under control of The Prophet would soon attack the place, and that they had been warned to leave. On the same evening at twilight the reports of four guns were heard in the direction where two young men from the fort had been making hay, about a quarter of a mile from the fort. Captain Taylor had been reared in Kentucky and had been educated in woodcraft by Lewis

SITE OF FORT HARRISON.

Whetzell, the celebrated Indian fighter, so he did not send out an investigating party that night, but at 8 o'clock in the morning a corporal was sent out with a small party, who soon reported finding the bodies of the two men, shot and scalped; and they were brought in and buried. Late in the evening of the 4th old Josey Renard (a Kickapoo, whose proper name was Na-mah-toha, or "Standing"—sometimes translated "Man-on-his-Feet"), appeared before the fort with about forty Indians under a white flag and announced that they wanted to have a talk in the morning, and to try to get something to eat, after which they retired. Captain Taylor was alert. He examined the arms of the men to see that they were in perfect order, issued sixteen rounds of ammunition, and, as the night was dark and the sentinels could not see every part of the fort, directed the officer of the guard to patrol the inside. He then went to bed, as he was just recovering from an attack of fever.

Through the surrounding woods a force of about 600 warriors crept to the cover nearest the fort in the quiet night. The attack was planned by a Kickapoo chief known as La Farine (a French translation of his Indian name P'kwaw'-shi-kŭn — Judge Beckwith makes it Pa-koi-shee-can—which is their word for wheat, and also for flour or bread made of wheat). According to his own story, he made up a bundle of dry grass, twigs, and other combustibles, which he wrapped in a blanket, and fastened on his back. Then, flat on his face, he crawled forward, with a large knife in each hand. He would stick a knife in the ground and pull himself up to it, and then stretch out the other arm. Very slowly, listening to the movements of the sentinels, and moving only as they went away from him, he crept on till he reached the walls of the lower blockhouse.

Here fortune favored him. The lower part of the building was used by.the post contractor for the storage of provisions, salt and whisky, and the cattle had licked several holes under the bottom logs to get at the salt. In these he introduced his combustibles, and with flint and steel soon had them ignited, keeping the flame under cover of his blanket until it was well started. Then he slipped back into the darkness.

About 11 o'clock Captain Taylor was awakened by the discharge of a sentinel's gun, and ran out and ordered the men to their posts. His orderly, who was in charge of the upper blockhouse, called to him that the Indians had fired the lower blockhouse, and he at once had the buckets filled from the well in the fort. But the men were few, and some of them feeble, and by the time the water was brought and the door broken open the fire had reached the whisky, and the blockhouse was doomed. As the barracks, which formed part of the walls of the fort, joined this blockhouse, most of the men thought they were lost, and for a few minutes panic reigned. Says Taylor:

"What from the raging of the fire, the yelling and howling of several hundred Indians, the cries of nine women and children (a part soldiers' and a part citizens' wives, who had taken shelter in the fort), and a desponding of so many men, which was worse than all, I can assure you that my feelings were very unpleasant; and, indeed, there were not more than ten or fifteen men able to do anything at all, the others being sick or convalescent. And to add to our other misfortunes, two of our stoutest men jumped the pickets and left."

But young Taylor had the same qualities that gained him the title of "Old Rough and Ready" in the Mexican war. He quickly determined on throwing the roof off of the barracks, where they joined the blockhouse, drenching the walls with water, and throwing a barricade across the opening made by the burning building. Having convinced the men that this could be done, they worked with desperation to accomplish it. Dr. Clark, the post surgeon, who distinguished himself by his bravery throughout the action, led the party that threw off the roof, and this was done with the loss of one man killed and two wounded. The spread of the fire was checked, and a barricade was soon thrown across the opening as high as a man's head. These moves saved the fort.

While they were in operation a constant fire was maintained from the fort, and the Indians poured in a heavy fire of bullets and an immense number of arrows. But they did not have the advantage they anticipated. The fire lighted up the surroundings of the fort, and they did not dare to advance to close quarters. They kept up their firing until 6 o'clock in the morning, when daylight made the guns of the fort more effective, and then withdrew out of range. But they drove up the horses and hogs of the settlers near the fort, which they could not catch, and shot them; and they drove off sixty-five head of cattle belonging to the settlers as well as the oxen belonging to the fort.

There were only two men killed in the fort. One was engaged in throwing the roof off the barracks, and failed to get down when directed. The other was firing over the pickets, and called that he had killed an Indian; and, as he raised his head above the pickets to look for his victim, was himself shot. Of the two men who tried to escape, one was killed about 130 yards from the fort, and the other made his way back to the gate and begged for it to be opened. Taylor thought this an Indian stratagem and ordered him shot; but fortunately Dr. Clark recognized his voice and directed him to lie down behind a barrel that was lying near the fort. He did so, and after daylight was admitted to the fort with a badly broken arm and some other injuries. In addition to these, two men were wounded, but not seriously.

The Indians engaged in the attack were chiefly Potawatomis, Kickapoos and Winnebagos, but Taylor says there were also a number of Miamis. A French interpreter in the fort asserted that he recognized the Wea chief, Stone Eater (Sā'-ne-mă-hŏn'-gah), and the Miami chief, Negro Legs (a nickname; his name was Mŭk'-kwah-kō-nŏn'-gah, which may be rendered "Bear Marks," as it means the scratches on the bark of a tree made by a bear in climbing). The Indian loss was never learned, as they carried their dead and wounded away with them, but probably it was not large.

Before night of the 5th Taylor had closed up the gap made by the burned blockhouse by putting up a strong row of pickets, which were obtained by pulling down the guard-house. The fort was now safe from direct attack, but was in a bad way for provisions, as the supplies had been burned; and for some days the inmates had to subsist on green corn, which fortunately was abundant. On the 10th Taylor attempted to send messengers to Vincennes by river, as none

DEFENCE OF FORT HARRISON.
(From the drawing by Darley.)

of his men knew the country, but they found the Indians watching the river, and were forced to turn back. On the 13th Taylor sent two more messengers by land, who succeeded in getting through, but relief was already on the way. News of the attack on the fort had reached Vincennes on the 6th by messengers who had started for Fort Harrison, and had been driven back by the Indians. Troops were assembling at Vincennes for the war, and on the 12th a force of 1,200 men, under Col. William Russell, started from Vincennes to the relief of the fort. They found no Indians, but a party of eleven men that followed them, escorting a provision train for Fort Harrison, was attacked at "The Narrows," in Sullivan County, and defeated, with the loss of seven men, and all the provisions. Colonel Russell left Colonel Wilcox's regiment of Kentucky volunteers at the fort, temporarily, and the Indians soon disappeared from the vicinity.

The gallant defense of Fort Harrison had a most cheering effect on the frontiers, and praises were showered on Captain Taylor and Dr. Clark from all sides. Taylor was brevetted a major by General Harrison, and his

regular commission as major followed on
May 15, 1814. He served against the Indians in the Northwest during the remainder
of the war, taking part in the expedition of
General Hopkins, and other movements, always with creditable mention. It has long
been felt that his service to this region has
not been recognized as it should be, and on
February 25, 1908, the Indiana Society of
the Sons of the American Revolution started
a movement to have the site of Fort Harrison made a national historic park. Its present owner, Mr. Ehrmann, is willing to dispose of it for that purpose, but for no other,
as he feels that, if not consecrated, the place
should at least not be desecrated. It is certainly to be hoped that the movement will
succeed and that Fort Harrison Park will
be handed down to future generations as a
memorial to American valor.

CHAPTER VIII.

THE PIGEON ROOST MASSACRE.

At the northern border of Clark's Grant, as you cross the spur of the Knobs, known as "the Silver Hills," into Scott County, you come to the valley of Pigeon Roost Creek. It was so named because there was here one of those notable gathering places of the wild pigeons that were so common in the Ohio valley in early times. Great forests of beech trees furnished their favorite food, and countless thousands of these birds gathered to nest and raise their young. They were so numerous and so easily taken that they were sold at 25 cents a bushel. Whether from the great slaughter of the pigeons, or the removal of the beech woods, the birds disappeared so completely in the last quarter of the nineteenth century that it was commonly believed that either they were extinct or they had migrated to some other country. But no evidence of any such migration has been found, and since 1899 their appearance in small flocks has been frequently reported in various parts of the country.

In this valley a settlement was begun in 1809, and, notwithstanding the troubled condition of the frontier, the settlers enjoyed comparative peace for some time. There were no Indians permanently located near to them, and the stragglers who came into their vicinity were not troublesome, and used to trade with them and hold shooting matches with them. Most of these settlers were related. Near the center of the settlement, a quarter of a mile southeast of the present monument, was the home of William E. Collings, a man sixty years of age, but well preserved, and an expert rifleman. With him lived his youngest children, Lydia and John, the latter thirteen years of age. A hundred yards east was the cabin of Henry Collings, a son. Three-quarters of a mile east was the cabin of another son, Richard, whose family consisted of a wife and seven children. Some two miles to the west was the home of John Biggs, and about three miles to the southwest was the home of Dr. John Richie, both of whom had mar-

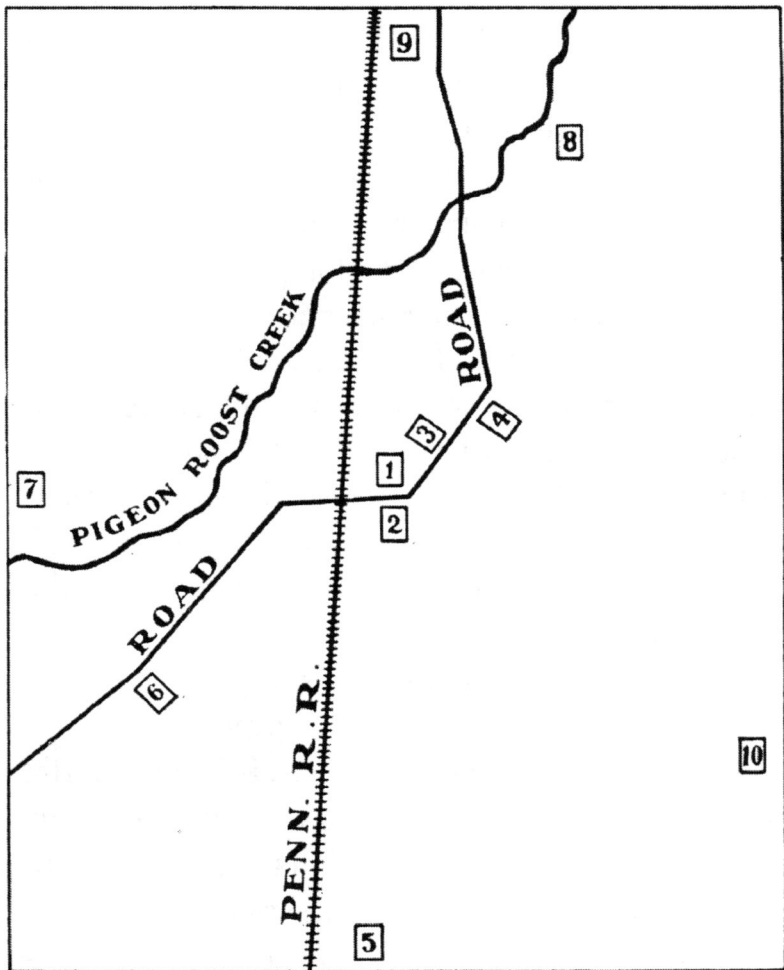

PIGEON ROOST SETTLEMENT.

1. Monument. 2. Wm. E. Collings house. 3. Henry Collings house. 4. Richard Collings house. 5. Zebulon Collings house, and block house. 6. Dr. Richie house. 7. John Biggs house. 8. Coffman house. 9. Jeremiah Payne house. 10. Silver Creek block house.

ried daughters of William Collings. Scattered to the north of the settlement were the homes of the brothers, Jeremiah and Elias Payne, Isaac Coffman and Daniel Johnson, who were also relatives, the last three having married three sisters named Bridgewater. As a measure of precaution there had been three blockhouses erected in the vicinity; one near the present town of Vienna, some six miles north of the Pigeon Roost; one about eight miles southeast of this on Silver Creek, and one five miles south of the Pigeon Roost, at the home of Zebulon Collings, another son of William.

On September 3, 1812, the same day that the hostilities began at Ft. Harrison, a war party of twelve Shawnees crossed White River at the present town of Sparksville, and stealthily made their way to the unsuspecting settlement. They first came to the cabin of Elias Payne, north of Vienna. He was absent, and his wife and seven children were speedily killed and scalped. Keeping away from the Vienna blockhouse, they passed on to the south, but on the way they tried to kill some cows belonging to Jeremiah Payne, and when the animals ran home bellowing, with arrows sticking in their sides, he realized the danger and hastily took his wife and child to the blockhouse. He then hurried away to warn his brother's family, but found the cabin in flames, while scattered household goods and strips of human flesh hung on trees showed that the Indians had accomplished their mission here.

The next victims found by the Indians were Elias Payne and Isaac Coffman, who were hunting bee trees in the woods north of Pigeon Roost. The savages crept up on them and opened fire, killing Coffman and wounding Payne, who fled and was pursued for two miles before he was overtaken and mortally wounded. His faithful dog, apparently realizing his master's helpless condition, returned to the Vienna blockhouse and attracted the attention of Jeremiah Payne, who boldly started out in search of his brother. Led by the dog, he found Elias unconscious and dying, and, having put him in as easy a position as possible, he went to get help, but on his return Elias was dead. They buried him where he lay, and the grave is still pointed out near the road, west of Vienna.

Moving on to the south, the Indians came to the home of Richard Collings, who was away on militia service, and his wife and seven children fell easy victims to savage fury. After scalping them and firing the house, they moved on toward the home of Henry Collings. He was working in the field when he was struck in the head by a bullet, and the Indians left him for dead. His wife had been to Jeremiah Payne's to get spools for warping, and was met by the Indians on her return. They killed her and with savage atrocity ripped her unborn child from her body, scalped it and left it lying on the mother's breast.

But now the Indians had reached the danger point. At the home of William Collings was Captain Norris, an old Indian fighter, who had been wounded in the shoulder at Tippecanoe and who had been sent to the settlement to urge the desirability of a block-house at this point. Mr. Collings thought it unnecessary, and while they were discussing the question they were alarmed by shots and caught sight of the Indians approaching the house of Henry Collings. They at once prepared for the defense of the house, where there were fortunately two rifles. Norris could not shoot well on account of his wounded shoulder, but could aid in loading the guns. The daughter Lydia was set to molding bullets. The boy John had started to drive up the cows and had caught a horse for that purpose, when he saw an Indian approaching. Dropping the reins he ran for the house, but the Indian was gaining on him when his father caught sight of them, and at the crack of his rifle the pursuer fell, while John safely reached the shelter of the cabin.

Collings took the other rifle, and as he looked through the cabin loophole saw a big warrior at the door of Henry Colling's home. It was a hundred yards away, but that was easy shooting for a frontier marksman and Collings was a good one, as the Indians knew, for he had often beaten them in shooting matches. He fired and the Indian dropped dead. The Indians now realized that they had trouble on their hands, and one of them tried the strategem of putting on the dress and shawl of Mrs. Henry Collings, and approaching in that disguise. But the keen eye of Collings detected the deception and his deadly rifle ended the life of one more redskin. After that the enemy kept carefully under cover, and apparently divided their forces, part going westward in search of easier prey and part remaining to watch the Collings house. But the occupants of this were alert and vigilant, and gave no opportunity for attack while daylight lasted.

After dark they realized that the situation was more dangerous, as the Indians might succeed in firing the cabin, and they decided to slip away from it and get to the blockhouse, south of them. The children and Norris went ahead, taking one of the guns, and Collings guarded the rear. The first three gained the adjoining cornfield without molestation, but as Collings passed the corncrib, an Indian who was concealed behind it fired at him, but without hitting him. He raised his rifle, but found that the Indian's bullet had broken the lock, and the gun could not be fired. He called to Norris to bring back the other gun, but Norris either did not hear or did not heed, and as the Indians did not attempt to come to close quarters, he made his way into the corn, where he became entirely separated from the others, and the Indians followed him. He passed through the corn and through the woods till he came to the vicinity of Richie's cabin, where he hid behind a log. He heard the Indians looking for him, but they did not find his hiding place, and at daybreak he started for the blockhouse, which he reached without further trouble. Meanwhile Norris and the children lost their way in the darkness, and after wandering hopelessly in the woods until they were exhausted they sat down to rest and soon fell asleep, notwithstanding the peril of their situation. When daylight came they got their bearings and found their way to the blockhouse in safety.

The defense of the Collings house, although the active part of it lasted less than an hour, served as a check that probably saved many lives, for evening was approaching, and the sound of the firing served as a warning to the scattered settlers. The Indians who went to the west found only one home where the people were not on their guard. This was the residence of John Morris, who was away on militia service, and his mother, his wife and his only child all fell victims to the tomahawk. The cabin of John

Biggs was found empty by the Indians. At sundown Mrs. Biggs had gone to the woods to look for her cow, accompanied by her two children, and carrying her baby in her arms. As she came near the edge of the woods, on her return, she heard the shouts of the Indians, who had surrounded the house, and at once started in flight to the blockhouse. The Indians fired the cabin, and finding that it was empty, entered the woods in search of the family; and at one time came so close to them that Mrs. Biggs heard their footsteps and their voices. While in imminent danger of discovery, the baby began to cry, and she was unable to quiet it in any way but by holding her shawl over its mouth. When the Indians had got out of hearing she found to her horror that the baby was smothered to death. For some minutes she was overcome by grief, but the necessity of saving the living nerved her for further effort, and, carrying her dead child in her arms, she slowly and painfully pursued her way through the woods with the two children until they arrived at the blockhouse, about daylight.

Others were even more fortunate in their

escape. Ben Yount, who lived east of the settlement, heard the shooting in the afternoon, and mounting a horse, with his wife behind him, and each carrying a child, the family went to the blockhouse on Silver Creek. Dr. John Richie also caught the alarm while working in the field, and hastening home, took his wife, who was ill, upon his back and carried her through the cornfield to the woods. Here they spent most of the night in hiding, and reached the lower blockhouse in the morning. Mrs. Betsey Johnson heard shooting and screams, and started to the blockhouse at once. It was none too soon, for she looked back and saw her house in flames, but she made her escape unharmed. Mrs. Beal, who lived near the settlement, and whose husband was away with the militia, heard the guns and fled to the woods with her two children. They hid in a sink-hole until after dark, and then worked their way to the southern blockhouse, where they arrived at 2 o'clock in the morning.

After Jeremiah Payne had made provision for his own family he mounted his horse and started to Clark County for aid.

Night had fallen, and the road through the woods was a primitive one, but as day was breaking he reached Charlestown. The alarm was spread rapidly and the mounted riflemen of the militia soon began to gather. A force was quickly started to the scene of the tragedy, under command of Major John McCoy. As they marched along they were joined by others to whom the call for aid had reached, and when they came to the Pigeon Roost about 2 o'clock in the afternoon there were more than 200 men in the party. Everywhere was desolation and horror. Only one house—that defended by Collings was standing, and about the ruins were mutilated bodies of women and children. The only person found alive was Henry Collings, who had recovered consciousness and crawled into a flaxhouse and concealed himself. He lived but a short time after he was discovered. At 3 o'clock the trail of the Indians was found and followed until dark, when the Muscackituck River was reached. It was too swollen to cross in the dark, so the party encamped for the night, and in the morning, having learned that the Indians started early on the preceding day, and probably could not be overtaken, the party returned to the Pigeon Roost.

In recent years a curious error has become prevalent, of writing the name of this stream "Muscatatack," though this form was unknown in earlier times. It is a Delaware word, compounded of Mŏsch-ăch'-geu, which means "clear," "not turbid," and hit'-tŭk, which as a terminal, in composition, means "a stream," and is usually applied to small and swift rivers. The proper Indian name is Mŏsch-ăch'-hit-tŭk—the "ch" sounded as in German—which may be translated "Clear river." There is no foundation for the translation "Pond river," which is commonly given for the name.

On their return the militia gathered all the human remains they could find, and buried them on the hill opposite the Collings house. On the next day, September 6, they were reinforced by a company of sixty volunteers from Jeffersonville, under Captain McFarland, and 350 volunteers from Kentucky. The united forces decided on a retaliatory raid on the Delaware towns on White River, but, owing to disputes over the organization, there being several men desirous

IGEON ROOST MONUMENT AND OLD SASSAFRAS TREE.

of command, the expedition was not made, and the forces dispersed. It was very well that they did, for the Delawares had nothing to do with the massacre, and had been friendly to the whites during the Tippecanoe campaign. Moreover, the presence of the militia was appreciated at home, for the whole region had been thrown into a panic, and a number of people had left their homes and gone to Kentucky. The courthouse at Charlestown was temporarily converted into a fort for the protection of the town.

But gradually the fear wore off and the people returned to their homes. Cabins were rebuilt at the Pigeon Roost, and work resumed, but the shadow of the tragedy did not rise for many months, though there were very few Indian depredations in that neighborhood thereafter. Zebulon Collings, one of the returning settlers, gives this vivid picture of their life while the dread was upon them: "The manner in which I used to work in those perilous times was as follows: On all occasions I carried my rifle, tomahawk and butcherknife in my belt. When I went to plow I laid my gun on the plowed ground and stuck up a stick by it for a mark, so that

I could get it quick in case it was wanted. I had two good dogs; I took one into the house, leaving the other out. The one out-side was expected to give the alarm which would cause the other inside to bark, by which I would be awakened, having my arms always loaded. I left my horses in the stable close to the house, having a port-hole so that I could shoot to the stable door. During two years I never went from home with any certainty of returning, not knowing the minute I might receive a ball from an un-known hand; but in the midst of all these dangers, that God who never sleeps nor slumbers has kept me."

So far as known, the Indians carried away only two prisoners on this raid. One was a little girl three years of age, named Ginsey McCoy, a cousin of Mrs. Jeremiah Payne. She was heard of afterward in an Indian camp on the Kankakee, and a party went to recover her, but the Indians had left, and no trace of her could be found. Many years later her uncle, the Rev. Isaac McCoy, and his wife, while on missionary work among the Indians, west of the Missis-sippi, found her the wife of an Indian chief, with several children. She had remembered her name, but had become an Indian in feeling. She consented to return to Indiana and visit her relatives, but after a short stay rejoined her Indian family for the remainder of her life.

The other was a boy, about 10 years of age, named Peter Huffman. He and another lad were in the woods, playing, when they discovered some Indians approaching. Peter hid behind a log but was discovered, while his playmate, who had crawled into a hollow log, escaped. Peter was sold to some other Indians, and was carried into Canada, where he was held for a number of years. At length friends got word of this, and William Graham, a member of the first constitutional convention of Indiana, went to Washington in his behalf. He interested Jonathan Jennings, then representative, in the case, and they secured the sympathy of President Monroe, who caused correspondence to be opened on the subject with the Earl of Dalhousie, then Governor-General of Canada. The Governor interested himself in the matter, and, by the aid of a Catholic priest who was well acquainted among the Indians,

finally succeeded in locating the captive
youth, who was returned in 1824. But he,
too, soon wearied of civilization, and it is
said that he went first to Charlestown, and
then to Jeffersonville, where he took passage
on a flat boat that was carrying a party of
Indians down the river, in their removal to
the west; and that was the last known of
him.

Of the Indians engaged in this affair,
practically nothing is known beyond this
passage in McAfee's History of the War of
1812: "On the 20th (September 1813) Lieutenant Griffith, who had been sent with a
scouting party to the River Raisin, returned
to camp with an Indian prisoner called Mis-
silemetaw, who was a chief counsellor to
Tecumseh, and uncle to the celebrated
Logan, but a man of very different prin-
ciples and conduct. He had been the leader
of the Indians at the massacre of the Pigeon
Roost, in the Indiana Territory. Griffith had
caught him asleep in a house at the River
Raisin. * * * He was an Indian of excellent information, and had been the constant companion and friend of Tecumseh.
Being under an impression that he would

now certainly have to die, he gave Colonel
Johnson a long and apparently very candid
account of past transactions since the treaty
of Greenville to the present day. He said the
British had supplied The Prophet's party
with arms and ammunition before the battle
of Tippecanoe; that Tecumseh's plan for a
common property in their lands had been
strongly recommended and praised by Colonel Elliott; and that the British had used
every means in their power, since the year
1809, to secure the friendship and aid of the
Indians in the event of a war with the
United States—having invited them to
Malden and made them presents for that
purpose; and having also represented to
them that they should receive British aid to
drive the Americans over the Ohio River,
after which they should live in the houses
of the inhabitants and have their daughters
for wives. He said he was convinced that
the British had deceived them, and that the
Great Spirit had forsaken him in his old age
for his cruelty and wickedness."

For ninety years the grave of the victims
was marked only by a giant sassafras tree,
over fourteen feet in circumference at its

base; but by act of February 11, 1903, an appropriation of $2,000 was made by the Legislature, through the efforts of the Hon. James W. Fortner, of Jeffersonville, for a monument to the victims of the massacre. On October 1, 1904, the completed monument, a fine shaft of Bedford limestone, was dedicated. It towers forty-four feet above the grave, companion sentry with the old sassafras, which is fast falling to decay; mutely calling to memory the most fearful Indian tragedy that was ever known to the soil of Indiana.

CHAPTER IX.

THE SERVICE OF LOGAN.

The name of Logan has three associations
with the Indian history of Indiana. The
first is through the Mingo chief, whose pathetic speech, "Who is there to mourn for
Logan?" has become one of the gems of the
world's eloquence. This speech was delivered to John Gibson, first Secretary and
some time acting Governor of Indiana Territory. When a young man, Gibson was
captured by the Indians, and was about to
be put to death, when he was saved by an
aged squaw, who adopted him as her son.
He lived with the Indians for several years,
married a sister of Logan and became
versed in several Indian languages. In 1774
he was with Lord Dunmore's expedition
when some Indians met it under a flag of
truce and asked that some one be sent to
them who could speak their language. Gibson was sent with them, and, having met the

Indians in council, he was called to one side by Logan, who gave him the speech as a message to the British commander.

A second Logan was a Miami Indian, known to the whites by that name, who was one of the victims of the Fall Creek murders.

The third was the Shawnee warrior, known as Captain Logan, for whom the city of Logansport was named. In the fall of 1786 a party of Kentuckians was led against the Shawnee towns on Mad River, Ohio, by Gen. Benjamin Logan. The towns were taken by surprise, most of the warriors being absent, and about thirty women and children were captured. After the first feeble resistance had ceased, the troops were annoyed by a discharge of arrows from some invisible foe, and on search found a boy concealed in the grass, who had undertaken this assault single-handed. He was promptly added to the collection of captives, and General Logan was so much pleased with the bravery and address of the youth that he adopted him into his own family, where he grew to manhood, and was married to a Shawnee girl, who had been captured in one of the raids by Colonel Hardin.

General Logan's son-in-law. He received
the name of James Logan and the name followed him when, shortly afterward, in an
exchange of prisoners, he was returned to
his people.

Logan became widely and favorably
known to both Indians and whites. He was
a fine-looking fellow, six feet tall and splen-
didly formed, with courage of the highest
quality. He was always a firm friend of the
whites, and on the breaking out of the war
of 1812 he joined the American army, and
acted as one of the guides on the march of
General Hull's army to Detroit. Soon after
he was intrusted with an important mission. The Indians in the vicinity of Ft.
Wayne were giving indications of hostility,
and it was considered desirable to remove
the women and children at that point to a
place of greater safety. John Johnston, the
Indian agent at Piqua, knowing Logan well,
and having great confidence in him, selected
him for this duty. Logan justified his
choice by bringing from Ft. Wayne to Piqua,
nearly one hundred miles through the wilderness, twenty-five women and children, not
only in safety, but bearing grateful testi-

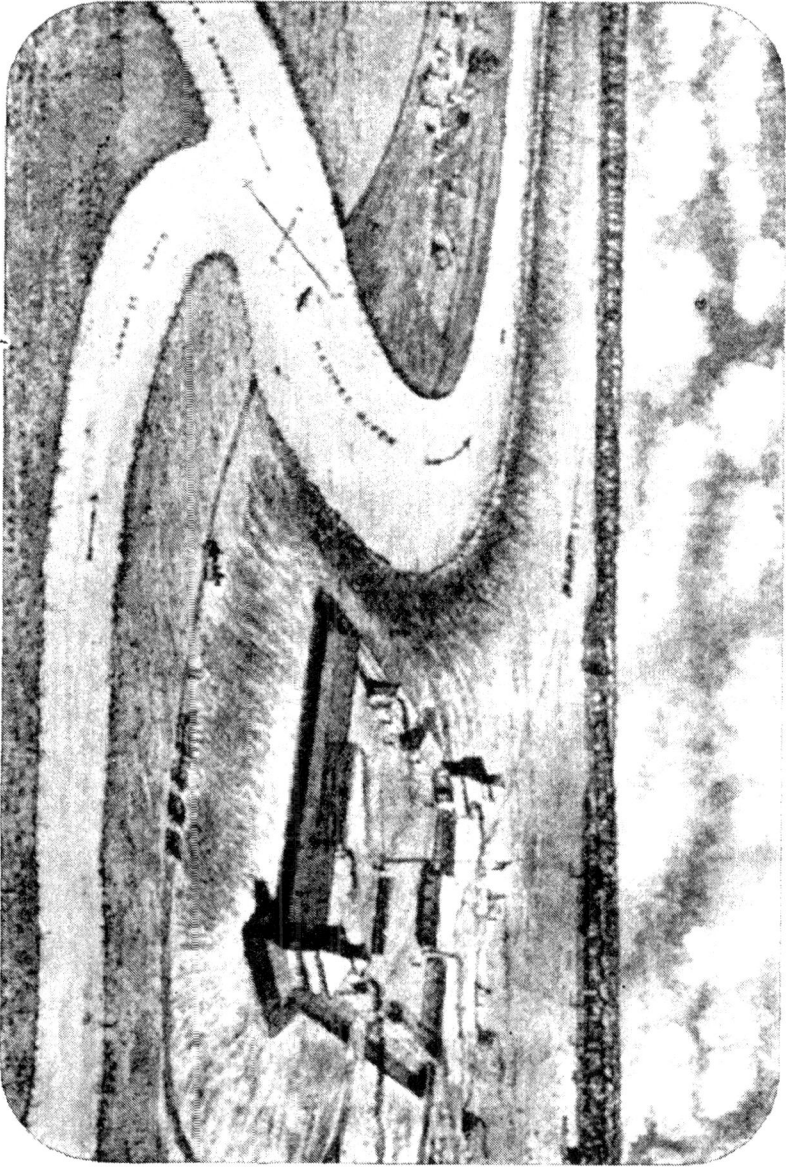

mony to his delicacy and kindness. It is said that Logan's sense of responsibility was so strong that he did not sleep while the journey was in progress.

The precaution was timely, for after the surrender of Detroit by General Hull on August 16, Ft. Wayne was soon invested by a force of about five hundred warriors. They pretended to be friendly, but secret information sent to Antoine Bondie, an Indian trader, whom it was the desire of Mē'-tē-ah (Kiss Me—a Potawatomi chief, who lived at Cedar Creek, nine miles above Ft. Wayne) to protect, put the garrison on guard. The situation, however, was perilous. There were less than a hundred men in the fort, and only two-thirds of them were fit for duty. The commandant, Captain Rhea, was old and was made completely incompetent by intemperance. The Indians, finding no chance for taking the fort by assault, decided to try treachery, and a plan was formed by a celebrated Potawatomi chief named Winamac (Cat Fish—not the one who figured at Fort Dearborn—the name was common among the Potawatomis.) He gained the confidence of Captain

Rhea, and arranged for a conference with a small party of chiefs in the fort, on September 3. Their plan was to carry knives and pistols under their blankets, assassinate the officers in the council, and throw open the gates to their friends.

But meanwhile deliverance was preparing. William Oliver, a young man who resided at Ft. Wayne, had gone to Cincinnati on business, and, hearing of the siege of the fort, he joined the Ohio militia, and tendered his services to General Harrison for an attempt to reach the fort. Harrison warned him of the danger of the undertaking, but Oliver was resolute. He overtook the militia at the St. Mary's River, where they were awaiting reinforcements. Gen. Thomas Worthington, an Indian commissioner, who was with the troops, joined with Oliver, and the two induced sixty-eight of the militia and sixteen Shawnees, among whom was Logan, to start with them. In two days they had reached a point twenty-four miles from Ft. Wayne, but thirty-six of the party had abandoned them, and the force was not strong enough to risk an encounter with the besiegers. It was therefore decided that

Oliver should make an attempt to reach the fort, accompanied by Logan and two other Shawnees, known as Captain Johnny and Brighthorn.

They started at daybreak of September 3, well mounted and well armed, and proceeding cautiously, reached a point four miles east of Fort Wayne before they found any fresh signs of the enemy. Here Logan found places where they had recently been watching the road, and, abandoning it, they cut across to the Maumee, which they reached about a mile and a half from the fort. Leaving their horses in the brush they reconnoitered on foot, and finding no evidence of Indians between them and the fort, they remounted, regained the road, and made a dash for the east gate. They reached it without interruption, but found it locked, and none of the garrison at hand. The Indians had moved around to the west and south sides in preparation for their assault, and the garrison was preparing for the conference. Oliver's party slipped down the bank of the Maumee, and up again to the north side, coming around the corner of the fort as Winamac and his party of chiefs

came around the opposite corner on their
treacherous mission. They were completely
disconcerted by the unexpected arrivals,
whom they took to be forerunners of a large
force, and after shaking hands, and protesting friendship, Winamac and his party withdrew, and Oliver's party was admitted to
the fort. Quickly grasping the situation,
Oliver hastily wrote a letter to Worthington, detailing the need of speedy relief, and
while the beseigers were still in confusion
and indecision, the east gate was opened
and Logan, Captain Johnny and Brighthorn
were started with it to Worthington's camp.
The enemy did not discover them until they
were well started, and then attempted a
pursuit, but the Shawnees escaped them and
reached Worthington the next morning.
The arrival of Oliver's party was remark-
ably opportune, for it was agreed by the garrison that there had not been another hour
in the previous eight days in which they
could possibly have reached the fort in
safety.

Immediately after their return from the
pursuit, the Indians began a furious attack
on the fort, which was kept up for seven

days. Several times they succeeded in firing buildings with burning arrows, but the garrison always succeeded in extinguishing the flames and repulsing their assaults. The defense was resolute and vigilant, Captain Rhea was practically deposed from command, and his lieutenants, Curtis and Ostrander, aided by Oliver and Major Stickney, the Indian agent, took charge of affairs. Several days after Oliver's arrival, the beseigers gained possession of a trading-house near the fort, from which they demanded the surrender of the fort, promising protection in case of surrender, and threatening extermination otherwise. They asserted that they had been reinforced by a number of Indians and two cannons, with British artillerists. Meeting a prompt refusal, they began a furious attack on the fort, but the garrison was ready for them. Every man was at his post, with several loaded guns at his side. The pretended cannon were made of wood, reinforced by hoop iron, by some British traders who were with them. One of these burst at the first discharge, and the other at the second. Lieutenant Curtis, who was in command, directed the men not to fire until the Indians advanced within twenty-five paces. The order was obeyed, and in a few minutes the enemy retired in confusion, having lost eighteen killed.

Meanwhile General Harrison was coming to the relief of the fort with a force which grew as he advanced to more than a thousand men. The Indians tried several times to surprise him, but failing in this, they did not risk a general attack. Their last attempted ambush was at a place known as the Black Swamp, five miles south of Fort Wayne, but failing there, they fired the grass and retired past the fort. This was on the morning of September 10, and a few hours later General Harrison's army drew up before the fort, and the siege was ended. Captain Rhea was court-martialed, but allowed to resign. Several expeditions were sent out to destroy the Indian towns within a radius of fifty or sixty miles, which was successfully accomplished. The fort was put in a complete state of defense, and all available cover within musket shot of it was removed. In the latter part of September the army began its march down the Maumee toward the British and Indian establishment at the

Rapids, destroying Indian villages and property as it advanced.

On November 21 General Harrison sent out Black Hoof (Mă-kŏt'-tă-way-kah'-sha —the name is written variously, usually dropping the first syllable), the principal chief of the Shawnees, with about twenty warriors, including Logan, to reconnoiter in the direction of the Rapids. They encountered a superior force of hostile Indians, and were forced to retreat. The pursuit was so vigorous that they dispersed, most of the party going to Fort McArthur, while Logan, with Captain Johnny and Brighthorn, made their way to the camp of General Winchester. They told their story, which was generally credited; but one Kentucky officer expressed doubt of their sincerity, and this so touched the sensibility of Logan that he announced that they would give proof of their loyalty on the morrow. The next morning the three Indians left the camp, going toward the Rapids. They proceeded without incident until noon, when they dismounted to rest. Here they were surprised by a band of seven hostile Indians under command of Elliott, a halfbreed,

BLACK HOOF (MA-KOT-TA-WAY-KAH-SHA.)
From Portrait formerly in National Gallery.)

who held a commission as lieutenant in the British service, and Winamac, the Potawatomi chief who had figured so prominently at Fort Wayne.

Four of the hostile party were mounted, and there was no chance for escape. With quick grasp of the situation, Logan walked boldly up to Winamac, with whom he was well acquainted, and said that they had tired of the American service, and were on their way to give information to the British commander. After some parley this explanation was accepted, but Logan's party were disarmed and they all started toward the British camp. After traveling a while they so gained the confidence of their captors that their guns were restored to them, but later Logan overheard Winamac advising Elliott that the prisoners should be killed. He then determined to take the initiative, and the opportunity soon came when the party stopped to gather some haws. At a signal Logan shot Winamac and Captain Johnny shot Elliott. Brighthorn held his fire until the others had loaded, and then mortally wounded a young Ottawa chief who was with their captors. The firing now became general, and, as Logan leaned forward to shoot, a ball struck him just below the breast bone and passed through his body. Immediately afterward Brighthorn was shot through the thigh. It was then decided to retreat, and Logan and Brighthorn turned their horses and fled, while Captain Johnny covered the retreat. They managed to get to Winchester's camp, some eighteen miles away, in five hours, notwithstanding their wounds; and Captain Johnny came in safely in the morning with the Ottawa's scalp at his belt.

Logan's wound was fatal. He lingered for two days in great agony, but displayed such fortitude that General Winchester reported, "More firmness and consummate bravery has seldom appeared in the military theater." He had vindicated his honor, but at the cost of his life. Reparation was made as far as possible by burying him with full military honors. Major Hardin wrote that his death caused "sorrow as generally and sincerely displayed as I have ever witnessed" in the army, and with cause, for his services had been so important that the British had offered a reward of $150 for his scalp. As he faced death, Logan displayed much concern for his two boys, and left a dying injunction to John Johnston, the Indian agent, to send them to Kentucky to be educated among his friends there. Johnston tried to execute this request, but was prevented by their mother, who was backed by the Shawnee chiefs in her opposition to sending them so far away. The matter was finally compromised by attempting their education at the agency, but the facilities there were slight and the boys finally rejoined their tribe, where they became as wild as any of their kindred.

The Indian name of Captain Logan is usually written "Spemica Lawba," and translated "High Horn," but it occurs in other forms. In the treaty of 1817, provision is made for "the children of Captain Logan, or Spamagelabe, who fell in the service of the United States during the late war." The first word is the Shawnee "spŭm'-mŭk," which also means "above" or "on top." This confusion of vowel sounds is very common in Indian names, and is very natural, for the spelling is phonetic, and it is often almost impossible to determine the short vowels.

In the spring of 1828 there gathered informally at the site of Logansport a little knot of early settlers, and others interested, to select a name for the new town which had just been surveyed. General Tipton, who admired classic titles, proposed an alleged Latin compound, said to mean "Mouth of the Eel," which was the name commonly given to the place at that time by the whites. Another proposed Ke-na-pe-com-a-qua—the common form of the Miami name of Eel River and of their old town at the mouth of that stream. It is properly Kĕ'-nă-pē'-kwō-mă'-kwa, i. e., Eel, or literally, snake-fish, or snake water-animal. Others proposed various names, and finally Hugh B. McKeen, a son-in-law of Barron, the Indian interpreter, who had formerly been in the Indian trade at Ft. Wayne, proposed the name of Logan, in commemoration of this friend of the whites. The suggestion pleased Colonel Duret, who proposed that "port" be added to round it out, and by common consent the name was adopted. And so there was given a monument more lasting than stone or bronze to this Indian soldier who died for the people against whom he had fought as a child.

CHAPTER X.

It is not generally known that the most valuable pictographic record of the Indians of the United States was obtained in Indiana, from the Delaware Indians, who lived on White River. The Indians have three forms of language—the spoken, the sign language and the pictographic, the last named being their nearest approach to a written language.

The second and third differ from the first in that it is in words, like our own language, while in them the signs, whether made by the hands, arms or head, or inscribed on some material, are ideographic. They are also universal, because they are "natural" signs of ideas, and for this reason, although the illustrations given herewith may seem unintelligible to us who are not familiar with idea signs, the Indians of different tribes, having totally different spoken languages,

181

communicate readily with one another by the sign language, and also with the deaf and dumb. This has been fully demonstrated by the experiments of Professor Gallaudet and others. Of course, in the latter they do not use the common mode of the deaf and dumb, of spelling out words with letters, but use the general idea signs which the deaf and dumb all use to some extent. Indeed, we all use them to some extent, as in shaking or nodding the head.

In summer, any boy knows what another boy means when he holds up a hand with the first and second fingers extended like a V. That is the natural sign for a valley, and the contracted sign for a stream. The Indians complete it in the latter sense by bringing a finger tip of the other hand to the crotch of the V, and moving it away in a wavy line, indicating the flow of a stream through its channel. From this comes the common boy's sign for going swimming.

The name of this Delaware record "Walam Olum" indicates the character of the record. In the Delaware language, "walam" means paint, and "olum" means a record stick, on which the record usually

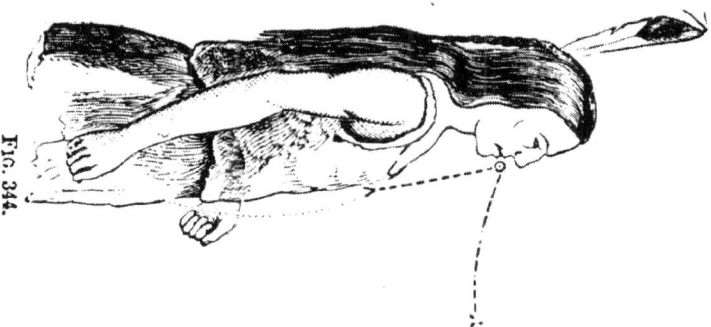

Fig. 344.

Word or idea expressed by sign:
A lie.

Touch the left breast over the heart, and pass the hand forward from the mouth, the two first fingers only being extended and slightly separated (I₁, 1—with thumb resting on third finger, Fig. 344 *a*), Fig. 344.

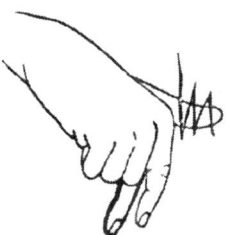

L 1, Fig. 344*a*.

CONCEPTION OR ORIGIN.

Double-tongued.

ILLUSTRATION OF INDIAN SIGN LANGUAGE.

was made by notches. Hence, the name means the painted stick record, or, as it has sometimes been translated, "Painted Records," or "Painted Sticks," or, as Professor Brinton suggests, "The Red Score," because walam is sometimes used specially for red paint, or vermilion.

For the preservation of these pictographs, the world is indebted to the celebrated Rafinesque (Constantine Samuel Rafinesque-Schmaltz), whose name is somewhat familiar in Indiana, because he was one of the most picturesque of the characters attracted to New Harmony. He was of French-German parentage, but was born in Turkey, in 1784. He was in the United States from 1802 to 1805, and returned in 1815, living here till his death in 1842. He was an all-round scientist, who published a large amount of matter, but was discredited by contemporary scientists, who doubted his remarkable discoveries, and it is only in recent years that the real value of his work has been recognized. And this is what happened as to the Walam Olum, for it was not until after his death that it was given to the public.

Rafinesque says that the original record was obtained from the Delaware Indians on White River by Dr. Ward, presumably a Kentucky physician of that name with whom he was on terms of friendship while professor of history and natural sciences at Transylvania University from 1819 to 1826. It was given to Dr. Ward in 1820 for important medical services, and in 1822 he obtained the Delaware text or translation of the pictographs. The English translation was obtained some years later by Rafinesque himself, by the aid of John Burns, an interpreter.

After Rafinesque's death it passed into the hands of Brantz Mayer, of Baltimore, and later to E. G. Squier, the distinguished archæologist. In 1848 Squier read a paper on the record before the New York Historical Society, which was published in the American Review for February, 1849, and has since been reproduced in Beach's "Indian Miscellany," and in Drake's "Aboriginal Races of North America." A complete reproduction of the pictographs and translations will be found in Brinton's "The Lenape and Their Legends."

The record begins with an account of the creation of the world, which is followed by an account of the deluge, and this by the story of the Delaware nation and its various chiefs. The opening words are as follows:

1. At first, in that place, at all times, above the earth.

2. On the earth was an extended fog, and there the great Manito was.

3. At first, forever, lost in space, everywhere, the great Manito was.

4. He made the extended land and the sky.

5. He made the sun, the moon, the stars.

6. He made them all to move evenly.

7. Then the wind blew violently, and it cleared, and the water flowed off far and strong.

8. And groups of islands grew newly, and there remained.

This is so similar to the first chapter of Genesis that one might naturally suppose it the source of the ideas, but archæologists agree that the Walam Olum is an entirely independent and original record. Its language is not "missionary Delaware," but of an earlier character; and the line of thought quickly leaves the Bible line. The great Manito (Kitanito) made only the things that were good for mankind; and then came an evil Manito—Maskanako, the great serpent—who made all the bad things, mosquitoes, gnats and flies; he brought quarreling and unhappiness, and bad weather, and sickness and death; and then, to cap the climax, he brought a great flood to drown man and the other animals. But his evil design was thwarted by Nanabush, an Algonquian deity who was a sort of patron saint of men, who created the great turtle and gathered man and the animals on its back, with the aid of the Manito daughter (Manito-dasin) until the deluge subsided, as recounted in the accompanying extract. The picture record brings the history down to the discovery of America and ends with these words:

"At this time, from north, and south, the whites came.

"They are peaceful, they have great things; who are they?"

But there is another chapter of the Delaware text, bringing the story down to the removal of the Delawares from Indiana, in

1820, written by one of the Indiana Delawares, and as one of the earliest known productions of an Indiana author is of special note. It is as follows:

SONG VI—THE MODERN CHRONICLE.

1. Alas, alas! We now know who they are, these Wapsinis (East people), who came out of the sea to rob us of our lands. Starving wretches! they came with. smiles, but soon became snakes (or enemies).

2. The Walumolum was made by Lekhibit (The Writer) to record our glory. Shall I write another to record our fall? No! Our foes have taken care
. to do that; but I speak what they know not or conceal.

3. We have had many other chiefs since that unhappy time. There were three before the friendly Mikwon (Miquon or Penn) came. Mattanikum (Not Strong)* was chief when the Winakoli (Swedes) came to Winaki; Nahumen (Raccoon) when the Sinalwi (Dutch) came, and Ikwahon (Fond-of-Women)

*Note by Raflnesque· "Mattanlkum was chief in 1645 He is called Matta-horn by Holm, who, by a blunder, has n ade his name half Swedish Horn is not Lenapi. Mattanikum means Not-horned, without horns, emblem of having little strength,"

when the Yankwis (English) came.
Miquon (Penn) and his friends came
soon after.

4. They were all received and fed with
corn; but no land was ever sold to
them; we never sold any land. They
were allowed to dwell with us, to build
houses and plant corn, as friends and
allies. Because they were hungry and
we thought them children of Gishaki
(or sun land), and not serpents and
children of serpents.

5. And they were traders, bringing fine
new tools, and weapons, and cloth,
and beads, for which we gave them
skins and shells and corn. And we
liked them and the things they brought,
for we thought them good and made
by the children of Gishaki.

6. But they brought also fire-guns, and
fire-waters, which burned and killed,
also baubles and trinkets of no use,
for we had better ones before.

7. After Mikwon, came the sons of Do-
lojo-Sakima (King George), who said
more land, more land we must have,
and no limit could be put to their steps.

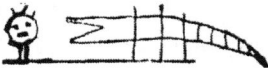

11. Amanganek makdopannek alendyuwek metzipannek.

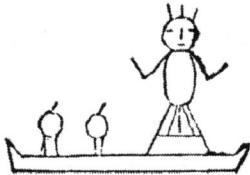

12. Manito-dasin mokol-wiche-map,
Palpal payat payat wemiche-map.

13. Nanaboush Nanaboush we-mimokom,
Winimokom linnimokom tu-lamokom.

14. Linapi-ma tulapi-ma tulape-wi tapitawi.

15. Wishanem tulpewi pataman tulpewi poniton wuliton.

16. Kshipehelen penkwihilen,
Kwamipokho sitwalikho,
Maskan wagan palliwi pal-liwi

SAMPLE. PAGE

190

11 There were many monster fishes, which ate some of them.

12 The Manito daughter, coming, helped with her canoe, helped all, as they came and came.

13 [And also] Nanabush, Nanabush, the grandfather of all, the grandfather of beings, the grandfather of men, the grandfather of the turtle.

14. The men then were together on the turtle, like to turtles.

15. Frightened on the turtle, they prayed on the turtle that what was spoiled should be restored

16. The water ran off, the earth dried, the lakes were at rest, all was silent, and the mighty snake departed.

OF THE WALAM OLUM.

8. But in the north were the children of Lowi-Sakima (King Louis), who were our good friends, friends of our friends, foes of our foes, yet with Dolojo wished always to war.

9. We had three chiefs after Mikwon came—Skalich, who was another Tamenend, and Sasunam-Wikwikhon (Our-uncle-the-builder), and Tutami (Beaver-taker), who was killed by a Yankwako (English snake), and then we vowed revenge.

10. Netatawis (First-new-being) became chief of all the nations in the west. Again at Talligewink (Ohio, or place of Tallegwi) on the River Cuyahoga, near our old friends, the Talamatans. And he called 'on all them of the east (to go to war).

11. But Tadeskung was chief in the east at Mahoning, and was bribed by Yankwis; then he was burnt in his cabin, and many of our people were killed at Hickory (Lancaster) by the land-robber Yankwis.

12. Then we joined Lowi in war against the Yankwis; but they were strong,

and they took Lowanaki (North-land, Canada) from Lowi, and came to us in Talegawink, when peace was made, and we called them Kichikani (Big knives).

13. Then Alimi (White eyes) and Gelelenund (Buck-killer) were chiefs, and all the nations near us were friends, and our grandchildren again.

14. When the Eastern fires began to resist Dolojo, they said we should be another fire with them. But they killed our chief Unamiwi (the Turtle) and our brothers on the Muskingum. Then Hopokan (Strong-pipe) of the Wolf tribe was made chief, and he made war on the Kichikani-Yankwis, and became the friend of Dolojo, who was then very strong.

15. But the Eastern fires were stronger; they did not take Lowinaki, but became free from Dolojo. We went to Wapahani (White River) to be farther from them; but they followed us everywhere, and we made war on them, till they sent Makhiakho (Black-snake,

General Wayne), who made strong war.

16. We next made peace and settled limits, and our chief was Hackingpouskan (Hard-walker), who was good and peaceful. He would not join our brothers, the Shawanis and Ottawas, and Dolojo in the next war.

17. Yet after the last peace, the Kichikani-Yankwis came in swarms all around us, and they desired also our lands of Wapahani. It was useless to resist, because they were getting stronger and stronger by joining fires.

18. Kithtilkand and Lapanibit were the chiefs of our two tribes when we resolved to exchange our lands, and return at last beyond the Masispek (Mississippi River), near to our old country.

19. We shall be near our foes the Wakon (Osages), but they are not worse than the Yankwisakon (English snakes), who want to possess the whole Big-island.

20. Shall we be free and happy, then, at

the new Wapahani? We want rest
and peace, and wisdom.

A little explanation may make this more
intelligible. In the ninth verse, "Tamenend" means affable or agreeable—literally
beaver-like. The reference is to the celebrated chief who was the original of St.
Tammany. In the tenth verse "Taligewi"
should perhaps be Alligewi, though Brinton
thinks that the Talega were Cherokees. The
Talamatans were Hurons or Wyandots,
otherwise known as Delemattenos. In verse
11, "Mahoning" is the Delaware word for
deer-lick. In verse 13, "Alimi" is evidently
an error, as it was the name of George
White Eyes, a descendant of the original
Captain White Eyes, of the Revolutionary
period. The latter's name was "Koguetha-
gechton," which means "large white space
showing in the eyes." In verse 16, the
name "Hackingpouskan," according to
Heckewelder, should be Hackink Pomskan,
and means "to walk on the ground." He
was the chief who was charged with witchcraft by The Prophet, but defied him, and
escaped unharmed. In verse 18, "Kithtilkand" is William Anderson, and "Lapani-

bit" is the chief whose name is attached to the treaty of 1818 as "Lahpanihle, or Big Bear."

The extract gives a forcible presentation of the sad feelings with which the Delawares left their homes in Indiana, and their forebodings as to their new home in the West. They were not destined to find "rest and peace." They located first in Kansas and remained there until 1867, when the neighboring whites became so annoying that they sold their lands, and, with the consent of the Government, bought lands in the Cherokee country in Indian Territory. Here they did well until the Dawes commission apportioned the Cherokee lands in severalty, and, with the inscrutable intelligence that occasionally invades Indian affairs, made no provision for the Delawares, who had bought their lands of the Cherokees, with the consent and approval of the Government. Now, the remnant are begging Congress, and have been for several years, to do the simple justice of giving them what rightfully belongs to them according to our own laws and in conformity with every dictate of honesty and decency.

CHAPTER XI.

The principal tributary of White River in central Indiana is Fall Creek. The name of this stream is a translation of the Delaware name, which Chamberlain gives as "Soo-sooc-pa-ha-loc," saying that it means "Spilt Water." His translation is rather fanciful. Sok-pe-hel-lak, or sook-pe-hel-luk, is the Delaware word for waterfall, but the word for water does not enter into its composition. The stem "sok" (sook, sog, sohk) enters into the verb "to spill," but also into the verbs "to rain" and "to pour;" and its primary sense is the idea of emitting or pouring forth. Pehellak carries the idea of "swift-ness," "rushing," "tumultuousness." The name refers to the falls at Pendleton, which were formerly about eight feet in hight. In 1864 a milldam was made on the rock ledge, immediately above the fall, making an impressive double fall of it; but this has been removed and the rock ledge has been partially cut to drain lands above, and the fall is now not very striking in appearance.

The Miami name of the stream is Chănk'-tŭn-oon'-gi, or "Makes-a-Noise Place," and the unusual occurrence of a place name for a stream is due to the reference to these same falls. The site of Indianapolis, being at the mouth of Fall Creek, was also called Chănk'-tŭn-oon'-gi by the Miamis, and the name is also sometimes given to Indianapolis. The falls were noted among the Indians on their own account; and in the period of white settlement the place has become notable for two events that occurred there—the mobbing of Frederick Douglass, in the days of slavery agitation, and the conviction and execution of certain white men for the murder of a party of Indians.

After the Delawares moved west from Indiana, their villages on White River were partially occupied for several years by Indians from the northern part of the State, and their lands were common hunting grounds until the progress of settlement drove out the game. In the spring of 1824 a small party of Indians camped on the headwaters of Lick Creek, some eight miles east of the falls, and about a mile northeast of the present village of Markleville. There were two men in the party, one a Shawnee known as Ludlow, and the other a Miami, who went by the name of Logan. With them were three women, two boys about ten years of age, and two girls who were younger. The men were engaged in hunting and trapping, and the whole party was quiet and inoffensive. But they had been very successful in their hunting, and had a large quantity of furs, in addition to a good supply of kettles and utensils for making maple sugar; and their property excited the greed of a white man named Harper, living in the vicinity. He was a frontiersman of the reckless class, who often boasted of the number of Indians he had killed, and openly maintained that it was no worse to kill an Indian than to kill a wild animal. He secured the alliance of James Hudson, another trapper of somewhat better character, and these two took into their plot Andrew Sawyer and John T. Bridge, brothers-in-law, two settlers who were clearing farms near by.

On Monday, March 22, these four men, accompanied by Bridge's son John, a stripling of nineteen years, and a boy named Andrew Jones, appeared at the Indian camp, professing to be in search of some lost horses. The Indians readily consented to aid in the search, and Ludlow started in one direction, followed by Harper, and the Miami in another, followed by Hudson, the rest of the party bringing up the rear. After going a short distance Harper shot Ludlow in the back, instantly killing him. At the report of his gun Hudson shot the Miami, Logan, in the same manner. The five men then returned to the camp and opened fire on the helpless survivors. Sawyer and each of the Bridges shot a squaw, and Sawyer then shot the oldest boy, but did not kill him. The other children were killed, but it was not definitely learned by whom, as all the party were shooting. Seeing that the boy he had shot was not dead, Sawyer seized him by the legs and dashed his brains out on a log. The murderers plundered the camp of everything of value, and mutilated the bodies of their victims, to create the impression that they had been killed by Indians.

On the following day some persons on their way to a religious meeting in the neighborhood discovered the dead bodies and the plundered camp, and the news spread rapidly, exciting horror and alarm. Whatever prejudice may have existed on the frontiers against Indians, there was never any sympathy with robbery, for that was a danger to which all were exposed. For ten years there had been no Indian troubles, and everybody knew the tendency of the Indian to revenge. There were many Indians near at hand and few whites. There were a few houses at the falls, small villages at Anderson and Indianapolis, and scattered settlers between these points, most of the country being covered with unbroken forest. Capt. John Berry, who lived at Anderson, started at once to Piqua, O., and gave notice to John Johnston, the Indian agent for the district, who promptly notified the authorities at Washington. The Indian Department immediately offered rewards for the apprehension and conviction of the murderers, and under its instructions Colonel Johnston and

William Conner visited the Indians and assured them that the Government would punish the murderers.

But, meanwhile, the settlers had been moving. Parties were at once formed to apprehend the murderers, and suspicion quickly fell on the guilty parties. Harper managed to escape, but within a week the others were under arrest and had made partial confession, while sufficient evidence had been obtained to demonstrate their guilt. A session of the Circuit Court occurred at Pendleton in April, and on the 9th of that month the four prisoners were indicted for murder, but on account of the illness of the presiding judge their trials were set for the October term. Meanwhile the prisoners were confined in the new jail, a structure of hewn logs fitted closely together, with one door and no windows, and surrounded by a stockade of heavy posts set in the ground. On July 20 the prisoners all escaped, but they were soon recaptured, and after that they were heavily ironed and guarded day and night by a specially appointed body of men paid by the Indian Department.

At that time the circuit courts of Indiana,

were composed of three members, a presiding judge, who was learned in the law, and two associates who were not, and whose function was presumably to temper the law with common sense. The presiding judge was William W. Wick, a young man, but an excellent lawyer, who afterward became quite prominent in the State. The associate judges were Adam Winsell, the village blacksmith, and Samuel Holliday, both pioneers of excellent character.

The members of the bar used occasionally to have a little quiet diversion with the associate judges, and on October 7, the court having been opened in the absence of the presiding judge, the attorneys for the defendants asked for a writ of habeas corpus, for the release of their clients. After a somewhat perplexing argument, Judge Winsell disposed of the matter by saying: "It would do you no good to bring out the prisoners. I ironed them myself, and you will never get them irons off until they are tried, habeas corpus or no habeas corpus." On the arrival of Judge Wick the prisoners were arraigned, and asked for separate trials, and on the next morning the trial of

James Hudson began. The court was held in the cabin of William McCartney, there being no courthouse. The prosecutor was Harvey Gregg, a prominent lawyer of early times, and the Indian Department had employed to assist him Gen. James Noble, and his son-in-law, Philip Sweetser, both able lawyers. General Noble was United States Senator from Indiana from 1816 to his death, in 1831, and was considered the strongest jury lawyer of the Indiana bar. The defense was represented by William R. Morris, Calvin Fletcher, Bethuel F. Morris and Martin M. Ray, all excellent lawyers.

The jury was typical of the frontier. It was noted that every juryman wore moccasins and carried a hunting knife. The evidence was brief, consisting chiefly of the testimony of the boy, Andrew Jones. The facts were practically undisputed, and the defendants' attorneys devoted most of the day to the recital of Indian atrocities on the frontier, but the appeal to prejudice was of no avail. The case went to the jury that night, and in the morning it returned a verdict of murder. Hudson was called up for sentence, and Judge Wick delivered an impressive address, referring to the atrocity of the crime, the wrongs of the Indians, the duties of the whites as civilized and Christian people. He said: "I feel no wish unnecessarily to harrow up your feelings, but I must ask you why you could not permit Logan to revisit his former home, and to hunt in his native forests? How could you have the heart to make war upon, shoot and destroy the venerable old chief, whose name ought to have been his passport and protection from Maine to Georgia, and from the Mississippi to the Atlantic? The blood of a Logan has a second time gone up before heaven crying aloud for vengeance. The blood of a Logan and a friend of the white man rests upon your conscience, and has imprinted a stain too deep to be washed out but by the blood of a Redeemer."

Hudson was sentenced to be hanged on December 1, but his case was appealed to the Supreme Court, and a respite was granted him by the Governor until January 12. The other cases went over to the spring term of 1825. The Supreme Court evidently made no search for technicalities on which to reverse the case. It easily disposed of such objections as that the grand jury had been chosen by the clerk instead of the County Commissioners, and that the clerk had intentionally included men not qualified to serve as trial jurors. It hesitated a little over the fact that the defense had not been allowed to ask the jurors whether they believed that a conviction was necessary for the protection of themselves and their families from the Indians; but decided that, although such a belief would disqualify a juror, the juror could not be asked "to testify to his own depravity."

On the night of November 13—the same day on which the Supreme Court made its decision—Hudson managed to escape from the jail, and was assisted over the stockade by his fellow-prisoners. In his effort to elude the pursuit he waded Fall Creek where it was quite deep, and, as the night was cold, he became so chilled by his wet clothing that he was unable to go on. He crawled into a hollow log for shelter, but his feet were exposed and were so badly frozen that he could not walk. Here he was found, completely helpless, and taken back to jail. On January 12 the sentence was executed. The

THE FALLS AT PENDLETON.

scaffold was erected at the edge of the bottomland north of the jail. The neighboring hillside was covered with spectators from all the country round, including several Indians, who had come to see if punishment would actually be made. Hudson had to be helped to the scaffold, being in such pitiable condition as excited the sympathy of those who saw him. He made full confession before his death. This, it is said, was the first instance of a white man being executed for the murder of an Indian in the United States. Certainly it was the first case in this region. Men were arrested and tried repeatedly in territorial times for murdering Indians, but the juries always refused to convict, although by treaty we were bound to punish such offenders. Governor Harrison complained of this repeatedly in letters to the Government and in messages to the Legislature. It was the more shameful because the Indians either surrendered their offenders or punished them. In 1811, having demanded of the Delawares the surrender of an Indian charged with robbery, Governor Harrison wrote: "They said they would never deliver up another man until some of the white persons were punished who had murdered their people. They would, however, punish him themselves, and did put him to death."

The other trials came on in the spring of 1825. The circuit had been changed, and Miles C. Eggleston was the presiding judge, the other court officials being the same, except that Oliver H. Smith, later United States Senator from Indiana, was the prosecuting attorney. The Government also added to the prosecution Messrs. Polk, Finch and Veeder, while the defense was reinforced by James Rariden and Lot Bloomfield, both talented lawyers. The new courthouse had been completed, a log structure of two rooms, with puncheon floors, and the trials were held in it. The juries were of typical frontiersmen, as before. On May 10 Sawyer was tried and convicted for killing one of the squaws, but he escaped with a verdict of manslaughter, and a sentence of two years in the penitentiary. On May 11 young Bridge was tried and convicted of murder, but with a recommendation to the Governor for his pardon, on account of his youth, and the fact that he had been led into the crime by the older men. On May 12 the elder Bridge was convicted of murder. On May 13 Sawyer was tried for killing the Indian boy. The prosecution dwelt on the atrocity of the offense, and Mr. Smith, holding the bloody shirt of the lad before the jury, urged on them that, although the shooting of the squaw might be manslaughter, the brutal killing of the wounded boy could be nothing but murder. A verdict of murder was returned, and on the following morning the three men were sentenced to be hanged on June 3. It was a pathetic scene as the elder Bridge, gray and already bent with age, stood with his brother-in-law and his favorite son to receive the sentence. They were haggard from their long confinement, and dejected by the certainty of their fate. The tears ran down their faces and the crowded courtroom was filled with their groans and sighs. Judge Eggleston's face was pale and his voice quivered. The solemn conclusion of the sentence, "And may God have mercy on your souls," could scarcely be heard.

On June 3 the sentence was executed in the presence of a larger assemblage than before. Again there were a number of Indians in attendance. Sawyer and the elder Bridge were brought out first and hanged from the same scaffold on which Hudson had died. But there was an added horror. Sawyer was a powerful man and at the fatal moment, by a desperate effort, he broke the cords that fastened his arms and clutched the rope above his head. Then ensued an awful struggle, while the sheriff and his assistants pulled down his arms and refastened them. When both men were dead they were cut down and laid in their coffins and young Bridge was helped up the scaffold by the sheriff. The black cap was pulled down over his face. Then there was a stir in the crowd and Governor Ray mounted the scaffold and announced the pardon of the youth, which was received with a general cheer. But when his face was uncovered his blank stare showed that executive clemency had come too late. Reason had fled.* The approval of the spectators gave way to regret that the pardon had been delayed so long. Tradition has it that an Indian chief present was asked if they were satisfied and that he

*Bridges subsequently regained his reason and lived to quite a ripe age.

replied, "Indian want no more white man weighed."

There can be no doubt that these tragic events made a deep impression on the frontier, where they were the chief topics of conversation for many days. The crime was so cold-blooded and unprovoked that it aroused the condemnation of almost every one. There were then two newspapers published at the village of Indianapolis. The Indiana Gazette denounced it as "one of the most outrageous transactions that has occurred since the settlement of the State." The Western Censor characterized it as "murder scarcely excelled in atrocity by the savages themselves." The general sentiment was no less pronounced and even the respite of Hudson was openly condemned, in the popular demand for swift and full punishment for the murderers. The sentiment that was awakened was wholesome and there was very little occasion for complaint of lawlessness during the remaining years in which the remnant of the Indian tribes resided in the State.

CHAPTER XII.

Just above the city of Peru, on the south side of the Wabash, the Mississinewa river empties. Massissineway, the whites used to call it, and that is nearer the Miami name, which is Nă-mah'-chis-sin'-wi. The Indians translate it freely, "Much Fall in the River," but literally it means an ascent, or as Sō-wil'-lin-jish'-yah (The Open Hand) explained it, "a slope up, but not as much as a hill."

The name is appropriate, for it is a fine, rapid stream. Its valley was for many years a favorite home of the Miamis. Just below its mouth was a large Miami town, which the whites called "the Osage town," because there lived here an Osage Indian who was quite prominent among the Miamis. His name appears in treaties as "Osage, the Neutral," but the Miamis called him Wah-shah'-shie, which is their name for the Osage

213

tribe. Their name for the place was Ik'-kē-pis-sin'-noong, or the Straight Place, because the Wabash at this point is straight for about two miles.

Seventy years ago, following the Indian trail up the Mississinewa, you would soon have reached the home and trading-house of Francois Godfroy, a French half-breed, who was the last war chief of the Miamis. They called him P'lŏns'-wah, or more broadly Pah-lŏns'-wah, but there is no such Miami word as this, and, indeed, he had no Indian name. It was merely their effort to pronounce Francois, for they have no sound of "f" or "r" in their language, but substitute a "p" for the former and an "l" for the latter.

Still farther up you would pass the curious rock cliffs, where the river has cut its way deep in the Niagara limestone; and still higher, some ten miles from the mouth of the stream, where the hills begin to come close to the river, you would come to the Deaf Man's Village. It was not much of a village—only three log cabins, one of them a queer two-story affair—and was the home of a Miami chief named Shē-pah'-cǎn-nah,

ROCK BLUFFS ON THE MISSISSINEWA.

or The Awl, i. e., the instrument with which
the Indians punched holes in skins when
sewing them together. In his later life he
lost his hearing, and was then named Kă-
kip'-shah, or The Deaf.

To this village, one evening in January,
1835, came Col. George W. Ewing, an Indian trader from Logansport, cold, tired and
hungry. He was hospitably received at the
principal cabin by old Mŭk-kōns'-kwă (Little Bear Woman) the widow of Shē-pah'-
căn-nah, who was an old acquaintance. After a hearty supper they sat by the cheerful
open fire and chatted in the Miami language.
The other members of the household
dropped off to bed and these two were left
alone. The conversation became broken.
She was evidently agitated. He rose to
retire, but she said: "No. I have something on my mind. I am old and weak. I
shall not live long, and I must tell it. I can
not die in peace if I do not."

He sat down again, and a long silence followed, she staring at the fire, and he strange-
ly drawn by her crown of reddish auburn
hair, with a peculiar light brown streak at
the back of the head—remarkable hair for

an Indian woman. Finally he suggested
that she tell her story at some other time,
but she answered: "No, no, I may die; I
may die; and then I will have no peace in
the spirit world."

Then she told her secret. She was a white
woman who had been carried away from
home by three Delaware Indians when a little child. She could not tell when, but it was
before the last two wars. (The war of 1812
and Wayne's war.) She had lost her mother tongue, and had forgotten her Christian
name, but she remembered that her father's
name was Slocum, that he was a Quaker,
and that he lived on the banks of the Susquehanna, not far from a town where there was
a fort. She thought there were seven other
children, six older than herself, but they must
all be dead—she was so old herself. The
Indians had carried her far away, past the
great falls (Niagara) and on to the Delaware towns of Ohio, where she was adopted
as a child by a Delaware chief. Her foster
parents treated her very kindly, and she
grew up as an Indian. Once, when traveling with her adopted parents, they found a
wounded Indian lying helpless on the

217

ground. It was the Miami war chief Shē-pah'-căn-nah. They took him home and nursed him to health. He became the husband of Frances, and he was a good husband. She felt that she must tell Mŏn'-kyōt (Bald Head, the name given by the Miamis to Ewing), but he must not tell others; her relatives might come and take her away from her home and her children.

The old woman had acquired the Indian's dread of the white man's power, and it was for this reason that she had guarded her secret so long. Ewing assured her that he would protect her, and when she had finished her story she said: "There, now, I can die. Oh, you don't know how this has troubled me. Something all the time whispered in my ear, you must do it—you must do it; and now it is done. The great load I have carried over fifty years is off my shoulders. I am a free woman."

In the morning, having convinced the old woman that she would not be carried away against her will, Colonel Ewing resumed his way, determined on an effort to find her relatives. He had no clew to their location beyond the fact that they had lived near the

Susquehanna, and at a venture he wrote to the postmaster of Lancaster, Pa., reciting the facts as he had them, and suggesting inquiry through the newspapers for a family named Slocum, from whom a child had been stolen by the Indians about the time of the Revolutionary war. The postmaster was proprietor of the Lancaster Intelligencer, but for some reason did not publish the letter. It lay in the office for two years, when a new editor came in the person of John W. Forney, afterward well known to the whole country. He at once published the letter, and luckily it appeared in a special edition containing some temperance documents that was mailed widely to clergymen. A copy came to the Rev. Samuel Bowman, an Episcopalian minister, who had been stationed at Wilkes-Barre when young, and was familiar with the pathetic Slocum history. He at once forwarded the paper to surviving members of the family, and it came to them as a voice from the dead.

And well it might. It was in the summer of 1777 that Jonathan Slocum had come from Rhode Island with his family, including his father-in-law, Isaac Tripp, and settled in the beautiful Wyoming valley, at the site of Wilkes-Barre. They were Quakers, and by kindly treatment won the friendship of the Indians who came about them. They escaped injury in the fearful massacre of July, 1778, and were so confident of their safety that they remained in their home after most of the settlers had abandoned the valley or gathered in forts. But their confidence was not well founded.

On November 2, 1778, three Delaware Indians approached the house. The men were away, but two neighbor boys were near the door grinding a knife. The elder boy, who wore a soldier's coat, was at once shot by one of the Indians. Mrs. Slocum and most of the children fled to the woods. Frances, a girl of five years, and a lame brother took refuge beneath the staircase in the house. The Indians went through the house and took a few things that attracted their desires. Then, noticing the children beneath the stairs, they pulled them out and started away with them. At this the mother's love overcame her fear, and, leaving the underbrush, where she had been concealed, she ran forward to plead for her children. When she pointed to the lame boy's feet the Indians abandoned him, but one of them swung Frances to his shoulder, and they all started on a run to the forest. To the tears and beseechings of the agonized mother they returned no answer but savage laughter. The forest closed behind them, the child looking back over the Indian's shoulder, with tears streaming down her face, as she screamed, "Mamma! Mamma!"

The alarm was given at the fort, and a pursuing party went out, but without success. The child was gone; and she had left indelibly printed on her mother's mind that last picture of her tear-stained face, and ringing in her ears those cries for help. And there was another source of anguish—one of those little things that sometimes wring the soul. Frances had a new pair of shoes, and in the usual economy of the frontier at the time she had been kept barefoot about the house until cold weather should come. Now the shoes stood useless, while the little feet were exposed to the stones and the thorns, and winter was coming on. Again and again she moaned: "Oh, if the poor little creature only had her shoes!" If she could

but have known it, Frances was quickly supplied with comfortable moccasins, and with
native dress that appealed to her childish
vanity as well as her sense of comfort. Indians are indulgent to their children, and an
adopted child is usually favored as much as
their own. But the mother could not know,
and to her came only the haunting face, the
cry of "Mamma! Mamma!" and the imagination of hardships of every kind; but worst
of all those poor, bruised feet, with no one to
care for them.

The days dragged by wearily, but her cup
of sorrow was not yet full. But six weeks
had passed when both her husband and her
father were killed by Indians while working
in a field near the fort, and she was left to
suffer alone. Imagination shrinks from the
contemplation of her woe, but in it all the
fate of Frances weighed most heavily. As
to the others the loss was hers, for to her
faith they were in a better and happier life,
but where was the child? There was no
peril, no hardship that her mind did not con-
jure up, for to her Frances was always alive
—alive and suffering. She must be found
and rescued.

THE DEAF MAN'S VILLAGE.

(From a painting.)

It was impossible to do much while the
war continued, but in 1784, as soon as hostilities ceased, two of the older sons pushed
forward to Niagara and made inquiry in
every direction for their sister. They
offered a reward of 100 guineas for her return, but if the Indians knew where she was,
they would not tell. In 1787 they made another journey into Ohio, whither the tide of
settlement had turned, enlisting the sympathy and aid of Indian agents and traders,
and offering a reward of $500 for their sis-
ter's return, but after several months of
fruitless search they turned back baffled and
disheartened. In 1789, there was a large
gathering of Indians at Tioga Point (Ath-
ens, Pa.), to surrender captives whose return had been demanded by the Government.
There the aged mother went also, braving
the hardships of the long journey through
the wilderness, that a mother's instinct
might not be wanting to know the child if
she should be there. But she was not among
the captives there, and the sorrowing woman
went back again to her life of dread and sus-
pense. In 1791, the brothers accompanied
Proctor's expedition to the Cornplanter's

town on the headwaters of the Allegheny, seeking for word of the lost one, but again without success.

In 1793 one of the brothers went to the Indian treaty at Buffalo, but returned with no tidings. In 1797 four of the brothers, with hopes renewed by the general pacification of the Northwestern tribes, went on an extended search, up through Canada and on to Detroit. They made inquiry everywhere and offered rewards. Even the Indians seemed to sympathize with them, but no trace could be found of their long-lost sister. Then, indeed, hope seemed crushed, and yet ten years later, having passed her allotted three-score years and ten, the mother went to her grave, still feeing that her daughter lived. It is not hard to believe that infinite justice and infinite mercy then lifted the veil, and let her know that her fears had been groundless—that her little girl, even among savages, had not been mistreated and had not suffered.

But the brothers and sisters did not know, and the dying injunction of their mother to keep up the search added inspiration to what had become almost a matter of religion to them. Letters of inquiry and appeals for information were continued whenever opportunity arose. Nearly twenty years after the mother's death there came to the East the strange story of the Wyandot mission—of the invasion of the Wyandot town at Sandusky by a lone negro apostle, without money, supplies or friends, who had finally learned their language, converted a number of the Wyandots to Christianity, established a Methodist church, and started the tribe on the road to civilization. And with this came a report that one of the converts, Between-the-Logs (Tē-ar-rŏn'-tū-ōs—he was of the bear totem, and the name refers to the manner of a bear crouching between two logs) had a white wife, who had been taken captive when a child. Possibly this might be Frances, and so, in 1826, one of the brothers, accompanied by a nephew, made the long journey to Upper Sandusky, only to find that their effort was again fruitless.

But even after this long series of disappointment the letter of Ewing revived their hope, and an interchange of letters with him almost assured them that the lost was at last found. Arrangements were quickly made for a journey to the Mississinewa by two of the brothers and a sister—all now over sixty years of age—and in September, 1837, they started on this last search. The details of the journey are not material. They came to the Deaf Man's Village, accompanied by James T. Miller, an interpreter, and James B. Fulwiler, of Peru. They were received by Mŭk-kōns'-kwă with all of an Indian's stoical show of indifference. Could this wrinkled old Indian woman be the fair child whom they had sought so long? Her hair alone appealed to memory. They asked to see the forefinger of her left hand. It had been crushed and the nail was gone.

"How did that happen?" they asked.

"My brother struck it with a hammer in the shop, a long time ago, before I was carried away," was the answer.

This brought certainty, for this had occurred about a year before her loss. She told the story again through the interpreter. Her memory of her father and the family, of the coming of the Indians and of her capture, all agreed with theirs. But her name was forgotten.

"Was it Frances?" one asked.

There was an instant show of emotion in her stolid face, which gave way to a smile as she finally answered: "Yes, Franca, Franca."

It was indeed the long-lost sister, but there were no tears of joy, no fond embraces. They told their part of the story, the mother's grief and the long search. They convinced her that this gray-haired woman was her sister who ran away to the fort with her little brother when the Indians came, and that one of these old men was that brother. She was interested, but she was an Indian as completely as if born one. She did not understand their language and they did not understand hers. The meeting was almost painful in its failure of anticipations, but the constraint wore off somewhat as they conversed through the interpreter, and she agreed to visit them on the following day in Peru.

In the morning—it was Sunday—Frances came to the new hotel in the little town, accompanied by the daughters Kē-ki-năk'-ish-wah (Cut Finger) and O^n-sah'-wah-shin'-kwă (Yellow Leaf), and the former's husband, Tă-quah'-kē-ah (Autumn), a French

half-breed commonly known as Captain
Brouillette—all riding astride Indian ponies.
They were dressed in their best, and brought
with them a ham of venison as a friendship
offering, which was delivered with due native ceremony. After some reminiscence,
the brothers and sisters spoke of the old
home on the Susquehanna, and begged her
to go back and make her home with them,
promising her every comfort in her declining
years. With a look of sadness she shook her
head and answered firmly:

"No, I can not. I have always lived with
the Indians; they have always used me very
kindly; I am used to them. The Great Spirit
has always allowed me to live with them, and
I wish to live and die with them. Your look-
ing-glass may be longer than mine, but this
is my home. I do not wish to live any better, or anywhere else, and I think the Great
Spirit has permitted me to live so long because I have always lived with the Indians.
I should have died sooner if I had left them.
My husband and my boys are buried here,
and I can not leave them. On his dying day
my husband charged me not to leave the
Indians. I have a house and large lands,

two daughters, a son-in-law, three grandchildren, and everything to make me comfortable; why should I go and be like a fish
out of water?"

"But won't you at least go and make a
visit to your old home, and when you have
seen us, return again to your children?"
asked one of her brothers.

"I can not; I can not. I am an old tree.
I can not move about. I was a sapling when
they took me away. It is all gone past. I
am afraid I should die and never come back.
I am happy here. I shall die here and lie in
that graveyard, and they will raise the pole
at my grave with the white flag on it, and
the Great Spirit will know where to find me.
I should not be happy with my white relatives. I am glad enough to see them, but I
can not go. I can not go. I have done."

Her position was supported by her daughters and Captain Brouillette, who was a man
of good habits, and one of the few Indians
who had adopted civilized methods of farm-
ing; and the brothers and sister themselves
finally concluded that perhaps she was right.
And so the meeting that had been dreamed
of for years came to an end. Frances went

FRANCES SLOCUM MONUMENT.

back to her Indian home, and the others
turned back to the East, satisfied that they
had at least performed their mission, and
complied with their mother's dying request.
There were letters, of course, and visits
from various Eastern relatives; and in 1846,
at the request of Frances, her nephew, the
Rev. George Slocum, came to live near her,
and give her his counsel and assistance. Most
of the Miamis had then been removed to the
West, under the treaty of 1840, but by a
special resolution of Congress, Frances and
her children were permitted to remain in
their old home. There on March 9, 1847
she peacefully passed away, and was laid to
rest in the little family graveyard on the hill
near by.

Half a century rolled away, but she was
not forgotten. Her story had become one
of the features of our frontier legends. In
1899 James F. Stutesman, of Peru, called
the attention of the surviving members of
her family to the fact that her grave was un-
marked. A family monument organization
was at once formed, and on May 17, 1900, in
the presence of a large number of whites and
Indians of the vicinity, and of members of

the Slocum family from all parts of the country a handsome white bronze monument over her grave was unveiled. As you look on it, and out over the valley where she lived, you are carried back to the olden time, and realize that this eventful life was one of the early links in the complicated chain that binds East and West, North and South, into one common fatherland.

CHAPTER XIII.

TIIE TRAIL OF DEATH.

When the Potawatomis made their last large cessions of land in northern Indiana, in 1832, they retained a number of small reservations for little bands that did not wish to go west of the Mississippi. Half a dozen of these were scattered along the Tippecanoe river, beginning at its head with that of Měs-kwah-bŭk's band, whose village was where the village of Oswego (an Iroquois word meaning "Flowing Out"—usually applied to the mouth of a stream) now stands. Měs-kwah-bŭk is the Potawatomi word for copper, literally red metal, or stone; but To-pash says it is also applied to a red sky at sunrise, and that it was in this sense that it was used in this chief's name. The reservation farthest down the river was that of Měh'-mŏt-way (Cat Bird. The word also means "He complains," or "he cries out with pain") and others, just above Rochester.

Other reservations were grouped about Lake Maxinkuckee (Mŏg-sin'-kē-ki—accent on the second syllable—or Big Stone country). Of these the largest was that of Aub'-be-naub'-be's band, southeast of the lake, covering thirty-six sections. Aub'-be-naub'-be is equivalent to our slang term "rubberneck," for it means "looking backward," as a person or animal looks back over the shoulder when going away from you. East of the lake was the reservation and village of Năs-waw'-kee (the Feathered Arrow—the word also means "a feather," or "one who feathers arrows"). North of these, at Twin Lakes, was a reserve of twenty-two sections for the bands of Me-nŏm'-i-nee (Wild Rice), No-taw'-ka (Hearing, or Listening), Ma-kŏt'-ta-m'wha (Black Wolf) and others.

In the year 1836 these reservations were relinquished to the United States by a series of treaties and most of the Indians were removed in 1837. The Indians were not very willing to go, and the treaties were the cause of much feeling. In Aubbenaubbe's band it resulted in the killing of the old chief by his son Pŭk-shŭk (Falling Down—the name is

sometimes written Pau-ko-Shuk). Pŭk-shŭk
was then made chief and started with the
band to the West, but escaped on the way,
and came back to his old country, where he
dragged out the few remaining years of his
wretched existence. By August 6, 1838,
most of the Indians had gone except Menominee and his band. Menominee had not
signed the treaty and refused to go. A council was held at his village, attended by Col.
Abel C. Pepper, the Government agent, and
a number of Indians and whites of the vicinity. Menominee was obdurate. When all the
argument had been completed, he arose and
said to the council:

"The President does not know the truth.
He, like me, has been imposed upon. He does
not know that you made my young chiefs
drunk and got their consent, and pretended
to get mine. He does not know that I have
refused to sell my lands, and still refuse. He
would not by force drive me from my home,
the graves of my tribe, and my children who
have gone to the Great Spirit, nor allow you
to tell me your braves will take me tied like
a dog, if he knew the truth. My brothers,
the President is just, but he listens to the

FOOT OF NASWAWKEE'S HILL, LAKE MAXINKUCKEE.

word of young chiefs who have lied; and when he knows the truth he will leave me to my own. I have not sold my lands. I will not sell them. I have not signed any treaty, and will not sign any. I am not going to leave my lands, and I do not want to hear anything more about it."

The situation was embarrassing. Menominee was an exemplary man—a religious man, who exhorted his followers to abstain from liquor, to be honest and peaceable. The Rev. Isaac McCoy, for eighteen years a Baptist missionary among the Indians of northern Indiana, bears testimony to this. A number of the band were also exemplary, for this village was the place of a Catholic mission, and the testimony of the missionaries can not be questioned. A chapel had been built in 1830. It was a log structure, thirty by twenty feet, standing on a little eminence on the bank of the largest of the four little lakes in the immediate vicinity. The west half of the structure was two stories high; the upper one, which was reached by a ladder from below, being used as quarters for the priest. It was of Indian construction, and not of the best. Father Petit says: "In more than one place we can see daylight through the walls. My fireplace is large enough to contain a quarter of a cord of wood. I have no carpet, and the boards of my floor are so slightly fastened that they yield to the pressure of the foot like the keys of the piano to the musician's fingers."

At this place, in connection with neighboring charges, Father de Seille officiated for seven years; and on his death, in 1837, Bishop Brute' sent Father Petit to take his place. Benjamin Marie Petit was a native of Rennes, born in 1811. After a brilliant course in college, he studied for the bar, and practiced successfully for a time; but in the year 1835 he felt himself called to the ministry in mission work. In this he was encouraged by Bishop Brute', who happened to be in Rennes at the time. He began his theological studies at Paris, and concluded them at Vincennes, Ind., his ordination being somewhat hastened by the death of Father de Seille. Father Petit at once entered on his charge, and soon became deeply interested in his Indian parishioners. He was not only a man of culture and deep religious fervor, but also of most tender heart and keen sympathy. His letters are full of praise for his Potawatomi converts. In one, written about a month after he had begun work among them, after describing their diligence in church duties, he says:

"Many are in the habit of frequent communion, and when deprived of this consolation by the death of M. de Seille, they practiced spiritual communion with the most edifying fervor. I have already baptized eighteen adults. The spirit of proselytism is admirable among these children of the forest; all the newly baptized, who belonged to another village, brought with them others of their friends in order that they might be taught their prayers and catechism. I could scarcely give you an idea of the attachment of my good Indians. 'We were orphans,' they say, 'and in the dark; but you appeared like a great light, and now we live. You take the place of our dead father, and we shall do nothing without your advice.' 'I do not hold the hearts of others in my hand,' said an old man, as he clasped my hand, while big tears filled his eyes, 'but mine will never forget what you have told us. If we have any trouble we come to you. What shall we do when you leave us?' "

At this time this was the only Catholic mission to the Indians in northern Indiana. There had been one for a time at the village of Chē-chauk'-kōse (Little Crane), on the Tippecanoe river, in what is now Marshall County, but it had been abandoned, and Father Petit's field included the Potawatomis of all northern Indiana and southern Michigan, as well as the white Catholics at South Bend and other points. He calls his mission "Chichipe Outipe," which I have not yet been able to identify, but the first word is apparently Shē-shē'-pa, which is the Potawatomi word for "duck."

Trouble soon followed the council at Menominee's village. The Hon. Daniel McDonald, who made personal investigation of the matter among the old settlers, says the origin of the trouble was "with Mr. Waters, who had settled in the reservation, without authority, a few months previous, and desired the Indians to leave so he could preempt 160 acres of the reservation, under the law of Congress passed in June of that year. He was the disturbing element and set about deliberately to work up the disturbance so that the Governor would be compelled to remove them." Certain it is that Waters claimed that some ten days after the council the Indians chopped his door and threatened his life. This was followed by the burning of ten or twelve Indian cabins. Then Waters and others petitioned Governor Wallace for protection. Colonel Pepper, the Indian agent, made a requisition for one hundred men to keep the peace and Governor Wallace at once appointed General John Tipton to raise that number of volunteers and take charge of the situation. He acted so promptly that, as Governor Wallace reported, "in about forty-eight hours after the requisition was authorized the requisite force was not only mustered but was transported into the midst of the Indians before they were aware of its approach."

This was true. Part of the Indians were in the chapel at prayer when Tipton announced his arrival by a volley of musketry. It was effective notice. Father Petit says of the old mother of Black Wolf, whom he found sick at South Bend later, "The poor creature had been so frightened at the discharge of musketry, ordered by General Tipton, when he made prisoners of the Indians, that she ran to the woods, where she hid herself for six days, without having any nourishment during all that time. She had wounded her foot and could not walk. Happily, an Indian, who was looking for his horses, found the poor fugitive, and, placing her on one of the horses, brought her to a French family near South Bend, where I heard her confession."

There was no parleying with Tipton. He was not a cruel man, but he understood that he was sent to remove the Indians, and he left no room for mistake. He says: "Many of the Indian men were assembled near the chapel when we arrived, and were not permitted to leave camp or separate until matters were amicably settled, and they had agreed to give peaceable possession of the land sold by them." The few arms the Indians had were taken from them. Squads of soldiers were sent in every direction to bring in stragglers, and by September 4 Tipton had gathered 859, young and old, for removal. It had not been arranged that Father Petit should accompany them. He assembled

them in the chapel for a final service, and
to remove the decorations. He says: "At the
moment of my departure I assembled all my
children to speak to them for the last time. I
wept, and my auditors sobbed aloud. It was
indeed a heartrending sight, and over our
dying mission we prayed for the success of
those they would establish in the new hunting grounds. We then with one accord sang
'O Virgin, we place our confidence in thee.'
It was often interrupted by sobs, and but
few voices were able to finish it. I then left
them." On September 3 the Indians paid a
last visit to their dead at the little graveyard,
and held an impressive service, accompanied
by general lamentation, that was indescrib-
ably pathetic, as they bade farewell forever
to the resting places of their lost ones.

Early on the morning of September 4 the
order to march was given, and the Indians
started on their long journey. The soldiers
destroyed all the huts and cabins to remove
any temptation to return. And now the
physical discomforts almost caused forget-
fulness of others. The season had been unusually hot and dry. The dust floated in
clouds. Many of the ordinary sources of

SITE OF MISSION AT TWIN LAKES

water supply had dried up, and others were almost unfit for use. Malarial fevers were unusually prevalent among both whites and Indians. On September 16 a Laporte County correspondent wrote: "Death, disease and drought are dealing distress around us. We had within a few weeks past more than four times as many deaths as in all the four years since the first commencement of the settlement of this county. * * * Deep River, through its whole length across Robinson's Prairie is entirely dry. * * * Cedar Lake [now a popular resort], a beautiful sheet of water two miles in length and one in breadth, has fallen so low that it has stagnated, turned green, with a very offensive smell that has affected the health of the settlers upon its borders most seriously. Cattle begin to suffer for food and water in many places."

For the sick and feeble Indians the rough traveling in the wagons provided for their use was almost unendurable. Even by the time they reached Logansport their camp was described as "a scene of desolation; on all sides were the sick and dying." They fared worse than the soldiers, of whom Tipton says: "I was compelled to discharge one or more every day and permit them to return home on account of bad health."

On they went through the Wabash valley, the suffering increasing until General Tipton united with the Indians in an urgent call to Father Petit to join them. His health was so delicate that his friends urged him not to go, but he obtained permission from Bishop Brute', and hurried after them, coming up with them at Perryville. He says: "On Sunday, September 16, I came in sight of my poor Christians, marching in a line, and guarded on both sides by soldiers who hastened their steps. A burning sun poured its beams upon them, and they were enveloped in a thick cloud of dust. After them came the baggage wagons, into which were crowded the many sick, the women and children who were too feeble to walk * * * Almost all the babies, exhausted by the heat, were dead or dying. I baptized several newly-born happy little ones, whose first step was from the land of exile to heaven."

And this was no exaggeration. A letter to the Terre Haute Courier, dated September 17, 1838, which was widely copied in the

State papers, tells of their arrival at Danville, Ill., and is notable for its tone of seeming apology for sympathy with the sufferers. The writer says: "Their movements are impeded much by sickness, and those various accidents to which an emigrating party of 800, old and young, may be supposed liable. Although there are fifty or sixty sick in the camp, this proportion is said to be less than that which exists in the county around Danville, and other portions of the Wabash, in proportion to population. * * * Some affecting scenes have taken place in the camp since and before the Indians were got under way. One chieftain had a mother upward of a hundred years old, over which a consultation was held whether or not it would be better to put her to death before she started, as no hopes of her long surviving (particularly under the fatigues of emigration) could reasonably be entertained. Fortunately, humane counsels prevailed, and the poor creature died and was buried after a journey of four days. * * * Others have been compelled to leave a wife after them in one place, and a child in another, in consequence of sickness; and some have had to bury, far remote from their native hunting grounds, or from the promised land of their adoption in the West, their nearest and dearest kindred. These things, of course, must excite one's sympathies, but how can they be avoided, considering all things? They are treated with all possible kindness by the amiable conductor and those under him; but yet, to see 800 poor, half-clothed, hatless, breechless creatures in a single file, choked with dust, and suffocated with heat, mounted on poor, half-starved Indian ponies, is a sight that no man of sensibility can look upon unmoved or with composure. The difficulty of finding water, horse feed, etc., in crossing the Grand Prairie, it is feared, may impede very much their march, as well as increase among them the progress of disease."

At this point General Tipton and his men turned back, except fifteen men retained as an escort, and the Indians proceeded under the care of Judge William Polke, the Government agent, and Father Petit. They rested for two days before starting on, and Father Petit records: "Here we left six graves under the shadow of the cross." Then they marched on into the parched prairies of Illinois, crossed the Mississippi, and on to the Osage River, where they arrived after a journey of two months over the trail of death, 150 fewer, by death and desertion, than when they started.

In his report of the removal, General Tipton says of Father Petit: "It is but justice to him to say that he has, both by example and precept, produced a very favorable change in the morals and industry of the Indians; that his untiring zeal in the cause of civilization has been and will continue to be eventually beneficial to these unfortunate Potawatomis, when they reach their new abode." But Father Petit was not to remain with them. He found Father Hoeken waiting to take charge of them, but he was so weakened by the journey that six weeks passed before he could turn back as directed by Bishop Brute'. One hundred and fifty miles on horseback brought him to St. Louis, but he could go no farther. He found kindly shelter with the Jesuits there—his last shelter. A month later Bishop Brute' received a letter from the rector of the Jesuits in which he said: "What a great loss has your diocese sustained in Father Petit! He arrived here on the 15th of January, reduced to a most pitiable state by the fever; eleven running sores on different parts of his body, his person covered with the tint of the jaundice, and in the last stage of debility. God certainly gave him strength which his body did not possess, in order to reach St. Louis. * * * On the night of the 10th of February they came to tell me that he was near his end. As I entered he raised his head, and inclined it, saluting me with a smile upon his dying lips. I asked him if he suffered much. He answered by casting an expressive glance at the crucifix, 'You wish to say', I replied, 'that He suffered much more for you?' 'Oh, yes,' he answered. I placed the crucifix to his lips, and he kissed it twice, with great tenderness. During his agony we recited the prayers for the dying, which he followed, his eyes constantly fixed upon us. He sweetly expired about midnight, age twenty-seven years and ten months."

Father Petit's memory is cherished. In 1856 the clergy of Notre Dame brought his remains from St. Louis and reinterred them by those of Father De Seille. One of them writes: "We consider these two precious mortal remains a double source of blessing for the ground they sanctify. It does us good to kneel between those two revered tombs, so eloquent in their silence. We feel very little inclined at any time to pray for them, but we love to recommend ourselves to their intercession." And the Indians are not forgotten. In 1905 Daniel McDonald, of Plymouth, who is thoroughly conversant with the story of their wrongs, and has called public attention to it, introduced in the Indiana Legislature a bill for an appropriation to erect a monument to the Potawatomis at Menominee village, and rebuild the Indian chapel. He made an eloquent plea for this memorial to the Indians we had mistreated, but his bill did not pass at that session. Undaunted, he continued his effort, and in 1907 his bill became a law. The commission provided for by this act is now preparing for its work, for which it is authorized to receive outside donations in addition to the $2,500 appropriated by the State, and in due time a fitting memorial will be made to these people, who, it must be confessed, suffered hard treatment at the hands of our forefathers.

INDEX GLOSSARY OF INDIANA IN-DIAN NAMES.

ABOITE—River and township in Allen County. A corruption of the French name Riviere a Boitte or Riviere a Bouette, meaning River of Minnows—strictly speaking, minnows used as bait for larger fish. The Miami name of the stream is Nă-kŏw'-wē-sē-pē, or Sand Creek.

AMO—Town in Hendricks County. Often said to be "the Indian word for honey-bee," which is ah'mō, in Odjibwa and Potawatomi. In reality it is the Latin "amo," "I love."

ANDERSON—County-seat of Madison County. Named for William Anderson, head chief of the Indiana Delawares. His Indian name was Kŏk-tō'-wha-nŭnd, which may be translated "Making a Cracking Noise," or "Causing to Crack." The name of the Delaware town at this point was Wah'-pi-mins'-kink, or Chestnut Tree Place.

ANOKA—Town in Cass County. Anoka is a Sioux adverb, signifying "on both sides," but in this form is used only in composition. As a separate word, the Sioux use "a-nog."

APEKONIT—Miami name of Captain William Wells, sometimes translated "Indian potato." It is the Miami name of the "wild bean," or "groundnut"—*apios tuberosa.* Pronounced ă-pē-kōn'-it.

ASHKUM—Reservation and village of a Potawatomi chief of that name, in Miami County. The name is variously translated "to continue," "more and more," "more of the same kind"—the idea being the same in each case.

ATCHEPONGQUAWE—A creek, tributary to the Salominee, in Jay County, now known as Butternut Creek, named in the treaty of St. Mary's (Oct. 6, 1818) to locate a reservation for the children of Langlois. The name is compounded of ăt-chē'-pŏng, the Miami for "snapping-turtle," and "wah-wē," an egg. Probably the latter should be plural, and the name would be better written ăt-chē'-pŏng-kwah'-wah.

AUBBEENAUBBEE—Township in Fulton

County, and reservation of a Potawatomi chief of that name. The name means Looking Backward, i. e., as a person or animal looks back over its shoulder when moving away from you. Pronounced awb'-bē-nawb'-bē.

BLACKHAWK—Postoffice in Vigo County, named for the celebrated Sauk chief Mă-kah'-tă-mē'-shē-kiăk'-kiăk. The name means Black Sparrow Hawk, but by universal usage it is made Blackhawk.

BLACK LOON—Reservation in Cass County for a Miami named Mă-kah'-tă-mŏn'-gwah, i. e., Black Loon.

BUCKONGEHELAS—Commonest form of the name of the great Delaware war-chief, and of the town in which he lived on White River. It occurs in many forms, ranging from Buckengelis to Pokenchelah and Packangahelis. It is properly pronounced Pŏch-gŏnt'-shē-hē'-los, and means "Breaker to Pieces."

CAKIMI—A Potawatomi woman for whose children the reservation on the Wabash River, below the Tippecanoe, now known as the Burnett Reserve, was made by the treaty of 1818. She was a sister of Tō'-

p'n-i-bē′ (Quiet Sitting Bear), who was head chief of the Potawatomis at the beginning of the last century. The Potawatomi pronunciation is Kaw-kē′-mē, and the meaning is "Run Away from Home."

CALUMET—Two streams of northwestern Indiana, tributary to Lake Michigan, Great and Little Calumet. The name is a corruption of what was formerly written Cal-o-mick, Killomick, Kenomick, Kennoumic, which represent dialect variations of the same word, varying from Kĕn-nōm′-kyah in the Potawatomi to Gĕ-kĕl′-ĕ-mŭk in the Delaware, and signifying a body of deep, still water. Calumet is not an Indian word, but of French origin.

CAYUGA—Postoffice in Vermillion County, named for the New York lake and city. The name is Iroquois—sometimes given as Gwa-u-gĕh—and is said to mean "the place of taking out," i. e., the beginning of a portage.

CEDAR CREEK—Stream in Allen County, tributary to the St. Joseph River. The name is a literal translation of the Potawatomi name Mĕs-kwah′-wah-sē′-pē. The town of the Potawatomi chief Mē′-tē-ah

(Kiss Me) was at its mouth, and took from it its name of Měs-kwah'-wah-sē'-pē-ō'-tăn, or Cedar Creek Town.

CHARLEY—A Miami who had a reservation in Wabash County, adjoining the city of Wabash; also a creek which empties there. His Indian name was Kē-tŏn'-gah—sometimes written Kē-tŭn-ga—which means "sleepy."

CHECHAUKKOSE—Reservation and village of Potawatomi chief of that name, on Tippecanoe River, in Marshall County. It is sometimes written Chit-cha-kos, and in other forms. It is the diminutive form of Chē'-chawk—the crane—and is to be translated "The Little Crane." There was for a time a Catholic mission at this place.

CHICAGO—East. Town in Lake County. There has long been a controversy as to whether this name means "Place of the Skunk," or "Place of Wild Onions," arising from the fact that the same stem enters into both words. The latter is certainly correct, as it is given by the earliest French chroniclers—Joutel and Lamothe Cadillac—and the Chicago River was known as "Garlick Creek" during the French period.

CHINQUAQUA—Reservation in Cass County. The name is a corruption of Shin-gwah'-kwah, which the Miamis apply indiscriminately to evergreen trees, such as the pine, the cedar, the tamarack, etc.

CHICHIPE OUTIPE—Given by Father Petit as the Potawatomi name of the Catholic mission at Twin Lakes in Marshall County, but not translated by him. The first word is probably Shē-shē'-pa—their word for "duck."

CHIPPECOKE—Common form of the name of the Indian village at Vincennes. The Miami name of the place was Chip-kah'-ki-oon'-gi, or Place of Roots, but the last two syllables are sometimes dropped.

CHIPPEWANAUNG—Place on Tippecanoe River in Fulton County, where treaties were made with the Potawatomis in 1836. The Indians say this means "Chippewa Place," but give no reason for the name.

CHIPWANIC—Tributary of the Tippecanoe, near Manitou Lake, in Fulton County. People of the vicinity give the name its proper Potawatomi pronunciation—Chip-wah-nŭk′. The word means "Ghost hole."

CHOPINE—Two Indian reservations, one in Whitley County and one in Allen County. The name varies to Chappene, Shappeen. It is a French nickname, properly Chop-ine, meaning a pint measure, that was applied to two Miamis. Old Chopine was Mă-kwah′-kyah, or "Beaver Head." Young Chopine was Pē-cŏng′-gah, or "Striking."

COESSE—Town in Whitley County. This is the Potawatomi nickname of a Miami band chief. The Miamis pronounce it Kō-wă-zi, and it appears in various treaties as Coisa, Koessay, Kowassee, etc. The Potawatomi pronunciation is Kŭ-wă′-zē, and the word means "old," or, as here, "old man." He was a son of Mă-kah-tă-mŏn′-gwah, or Black Loon, and a grandson of Little Turtle. His Miami name was M′tĕk′-kyah, meaning "forest," or "woods."

CORNSTALK—Postoffice in Howard County; also "Pete Cornstalk Creek," a small stream in the same county. These are memorials of an old Miami of the Thorntown band, who lived in this vicinity. "Cornstalk" was merely a nickname used by the white settlers. His proper name was Ah-sŏn'-zŏng, which means "sunshine."

DEER CREEK—Tributary of the Wabash, emptying below Delphi. It is called Passeanong Creek in treaties, and this name is still sometimes given to Deer Creek Prairie, opposite its mouth. This is the Miami name of the stream, compounded of ah-păs'-syah, a fawn, and the terminal locative; literally "The Place of the Fawn."

DELAWARE—Name of Indiana county, town and several townships, referring to the Delaware Indians. The word Delaware is not Indian, but refers to their former residence near the Delaware River, which was named for Lord De La Warr, Governor of Virginia. They call themselves Lenni Lenape (lĕn'-ni lĕn-ah'-pay) which may be translated "virile men," "true men" or "men of men." The western Algonquians usually called them Wah'-pinăch'-i, or "Eastlanders"; and sometimes

E'-la-nah'-bah, or "People from the Dawn."

DORMIN—Prairie in Laporte County. This is a corruption of m'dah'-min, the Potawatomi word for maize or corn. The name may have been given for a Potawatomi chief of this name, who figures in the treaties as "Me-do-min," "Mattaw-min," etc. The Odjibwa form of this word is Mondamin (spirit grain), and it is also the name of the spirit or deity of the maize.

DRIFTWOOD—Common name of the east fork of White River. It is sometimes said that the Indian name was On'-gwah-sah'-kah, which is the Miami for "driftwood," but I have never found a Miami who knew it by that name. On Hough's map it is marked "Gun-dah-quah," which may possibly have been intended for the Delaware gŭn-a-quŏt, meaning "long."

EAGLE CREEK—Tributary of White River, in Marion County. Chamberlain says: "Its Indian name was Lau-a-shinga-paim-honnock, or Middle of the Valley, so called from the beautiful bottoms that extend along it, sometimes from two to four

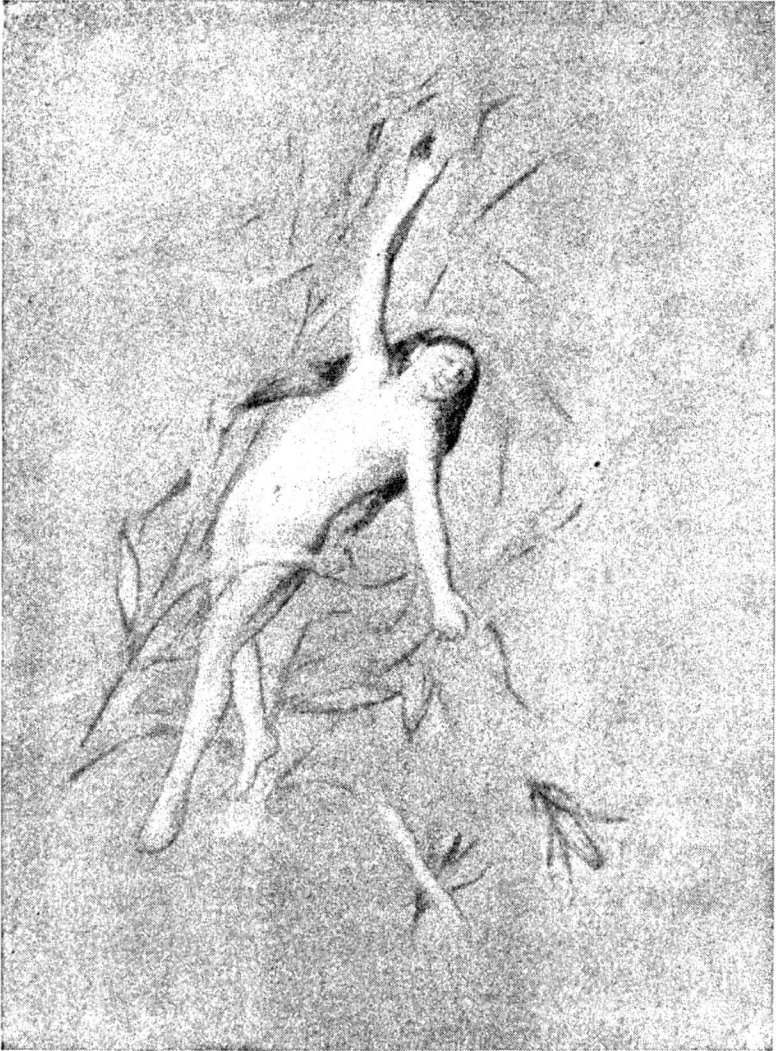

THE DESCENT OF MONDAMIN—SPIRIT OF THE MAIZE.
(By C. T. Webber.)

miles in width." This may be correct.
Lawi is the Delaware for "middle;"
schingeu means "level;" pem, or peem,
has the force of "near" or "adjoining;"
and hanni is a "river."

EEL RIVER—Tributary of the Wabash, emptying at Logansport. This name, and the
French name—L'Anguille—are translations of the Miami name of the stream
which is Kĕ-nă-pē'-kwō-mă'-kwa. The
final vowel is very slightly sounded, or not
at all. The valley of this stream was the
chief residence of the Miamis known to
the Americans as "Eel Rivers," who probably included what were known to the
French as Pe-pi-ko-kias and Miamis of
Maramech.

EEL RIVER—Tributary of White River, emptying in Greene County. Chamberlain
gives the Indian name of the Eel River
of the Wabash as Shō-a-maque, but probably confuses that stream, which was not
in the Delaware country, with this one,
which was; for shō-a-maque is evidently
intended for the Delaware name of the
eel, schach-a-măk, i. e., slippery fish.

ELKHART—Tributary of the St. Joseph's of

Lake Michigan; also city and county named for the river. The name was formerly written Elk Heart, or Elksheart, which, like the French name, "Coeur de Cerf," is a literal translation of the Potawatomi name of the stream Mē-shĕh'-wĕh-ou-deh-ik.' The same name was given to a Potawatomi village that was located on the stream. The name refers to an island at its mouth, which resembled an elk's heart in shape.

FALL CREEK—Stream of central Indiana, tributary to White River. The name is a translation of the Delaware name, which Chamberlain gives as "Soo-sooc-pa-haloc, or Spilt Water." Sokpehellak, or sookpehelluk, is the Delaware word for a waterfall, and the name refers to the falls at Pendleton. The Miami name of the stream is Chănk'-tŭn-oon'-gi, or "Makes a Noise Place," which refers to the same falls.

FLAT BELLY—A large reservation in Kosciusko and Noble counties, for the band of Pă-pă-kēē'-chi, of which the English name is a literal translation. The reservation extended to Wawassee, or Turkey

Lake on the west, but the chief's village was east of that, at what is now known as "Indian Village," in Noble County.

FORT WAYNE—Called by old Miamis Kĕ′-ki-oon′-gi, for explanation of which see Kekionga.

GODFROY—Reservation on the Wabash and Mississinewa rivers opposite Peru, to Francois Godfroy, a French half-breed, who was the last war-chief of the Miamis. It is commonly stated that his Indian name was Pah-lŏns′-wah, but there is no such Miami word—it is their mode of pronouncing Francois. He had no Indian name.

HUNTINGTON—County-seat of Huntington County. The Miamis call this place Wē-pē-chah′-ki-oon′-gi, or in shorter form Wē-pē-chah′-ki-oong, which means "Place of Flints." A flint ridge crosses the limestone here, which furnished the Indians a valuable supply in early times.

ILE A L'AIL — French name, meaning "Island of Garlic," for a small island in the Wabash, in Carroll County (Sec. 5, Tp. 25 N., Range 2 W.). The name seems to have been adopted by the Indians, and was used in the treaty of St. Mary's (1818), as "Esle a l'Aille," to locate a reservation to the children of Antoine Bondie.

INDIANAPOLIS—The Miamis called the site of the city Chănk'-tŭn-oon'-gi, from its location at the mouth of Fall Creek, and also sometimes give the same name to the city. It means "Makes a Noise Place."

ILLINOIS—French form of the word illiniwek, or "men," which was the name the Illinois Indians gave to themselves.

IROQUOIS—River, tributary to the Kankakee, and township in Newton County. Charlevoix says the word is a Gallicism derived from hiro, "I have spoken," a word by which the Iroquois were wont to conclude their speeches, and kowe, an exclamation. The Bureau of Ethnology derives it from an Algonquian word meaning "real adders." The name refers to an ancient battle said to have occurred on the stream, in which the Illinois routed a party of Iroquois.

JOSINA CREEK—A small stream in Wabash and Grant Counties, tributary to the Mississinewa. The word is an erratic corruption of Tō-săn'-yah, the common Miami abbreviation of Mĕt'-ō-săn'-yah, which is the equivalent of our word "Indian." Metosanyah's village was at the mouth of the stream, which on some maps is marked "Metocinyah Creek."

KANKAKEE—River of northern Indiana; postoffice in Starke County; and townships in Laporte and Jasper counties. Father Charlevoix gives the name as Theakiki, which he says the Canadians had corrupted to Kiakiki. This is the Potawatomi name, which Rev. Isaac McCoy makes "Tiau-kakeek," and which the Indians pronounce Tĕh'-yŏk-kē'-ki. It means "low land" or "swampy county." Father Marest wrote the name "Huakiki," which is a corruption of the Miami "Mă-whah'-kēki," meaning "wolf county." Both names appear on old maps. Kankakee is presumably a further corruption of Kiakiki. The name appeared later as "Qui-que-que," and "Quin-qui-qui;" the French pronunciation of the latter being practically the same as Kankakee.

KEKIONGA—Common form of the name of the Indian village which stood at the site

of Ft. Wayne. It is a corruption of Ki-
kă-kŏn, or Kis-ka-kon, which was the original name. The Kiskakons, a tribal division of the Ottawas, had a village here
before the Miamis, and the Maumee was
then known as Ottawa River. The Miamis corrupted the name to Kē'-ki-oon'-gi,
which they still apply to Ft. Wayne. The
Delawares made it Ke-gey-unk. Ki-ka-kon
means "clipped hair," and was given to
these Indians because they shaved the
sides of the head and trimmed the remaining scalp-lock like the mane of a Roman
horse. The French called them Queues
Coupees.

KENAPACOMAQUA—Common form of the
name of the large Miami town at the
mouth of Eel River, which was destroyed
by Gen. Wilkinson in 1791. The name is
Kē-nă-pē'-kwō-mă'-kwă, but the final
vowel is sounded lightly, if at all. It
means "eel;" literally "snake-fish."

KENTUCKY—Stream in southern Indiana.
The name comes originally from the large
tributary of the Ohio from the south; and
its meaning is uncertain, because the original form of the word is not known, nor

the language from which it was taken. In Henderson's treaty with the Cherokees, on the Watauga it is called Cantuckey Chenooe. But the name is also said to be Kain-tuck. John Johnston says the word is Shawnee, and means "head of the river." It was also called Cuttawa River in early times. Cuttawa is probably the Cherokee Ki-tu'-whă—a name formerly applied to the tribe, but later to a secret organization pledged to maintain the autonomy of the tribe. This was commonly called "the Keetoowah Society" by the whites.

KEWANNA—Postoffice in Fulton County, and reservation for Potawatomi chief of that name. Kē-waw'-nē is the Potawatomi name of the prairie chicken; and also means "lost." The word is very similar to the Miami Kē-wah-ni, which means "nose."

KICKAPOO—Creek in Warren County, named for the Indian tribe. The meaning of the name is uncertain, but Schoolcraft surmised that it was a corruption of Negik-a-boo, meaning "otter's ghost." The otter was one of their totems. They were closely associated with the Mascoutins, whose name is variously interpreted "Fire Nation" or "Prairie Nation," on account of the similarity of the words for "fire" and "prairie" in the Algonquian dialects.

KITHTIPPECANUNK—Popular form of the name of The Prophet's Town, and the old Indian town that stood at the same place. It means "Tippecanoe Town," and is formed by adding the terminal locative to the name of the Tippecanoe River, which is Kē-tăp'-kwŏn in Miami, and Kē-tăp-ē-kŏn in Potawatomi; and these are names of the buffalo fish.

KILLBUCK—Creek in Madison County; also Delaware village on White River, commonly known as "Buck's town," and named for Charles Killbuck, who lived there. Killbuck has become a Delaware family name, the original bearer of which died about 1776. His son, who was known both as Killbuck and Gelelemend (The Leader), was very prominent in Revolutionary times. He became a Moravian convert, and was baptised William Henry, in honor of a friend of his father. He died at Pittsburg in 1811, aged 80 years.

KILSOKWA—The oldest Indian living in Indiana in 1908, born in 1810. She is a daughter of Wahk-shin′-gah (The Crescent Moon—literally Lying Crooked), who was a son of Little Turtle. Her mother's name was Nah-wă′-kah-mō′-kwă, which she translates "The First Snow"—literally it means the one that comes first in anything. She says her own name means "The Setting Sun," but literally it appears to mean only "The Sun (feminine)," or "Sun Woman." Kil-sō′-kwă married a Frenchman, Antoine Revarre, and now lives near Roanoke with her son Antony Revarre, whose Indian name is Wah′-pi-mŏn′-gwah, or White Loon.

KOKOMO—County seat of Howard County; also a creek near it. Said to have been the name of a Miami chief of the Thorntown band, but there is no such name signed to any treaty unless it be "Co-come-wah," which appears in the treaty of 1834. It has been translated "Black Walnut," "Bear Chief," and "Young Grandmother," for none of which is there any basis. Both Godfroy and Kilsokwa say there was a Thorntown Indian named Kō-kah′-mah, and that the name refers to him. Godfroy says this name means "He Goes Under," as in diving; and that it may be translated "Something Diving," or "The Diver."

LAGRO—Town in Wabash County. The name is a corruption of Le Gros, the French nickname of a Miami chief who lived here. His Miami name was O-sah'-mō-nēē, which is presumably a Miami corruption of ōⁿ'-sah-lă'-mō-nēē—the Miami name of the bloodroot, and the original name of the Salamonie River, which empties opposite the town. See Salamonie.

LITTLE DEER CREEK—Stream in Miami County. The Miami name is Ah-păs'-syah, which is their word for a fawn.

LITTLE MUNSEE—A Delaware town on White River, about 4 miles east of Anderson (S. E. 1-4 of Sec. 17, Range 8 E.). It was located on the site of the old Moravian Mission. For meaning of name, see "Muncie."

LITTLE RIVER—Tributary of the Wabash, to which portage was made from the Maumee, in going to the Wabash. The Miami name of the stream is Paw-wē'-kŏm-sē-pē, which means "Standing Still River," or "No Current River." It runs through a flat country, and its natural quiet was increased by beaver dams, which travelers sometimes used as locks.

LOGANSPORT—County seat of Cass County, named for Captain Logan, a Shawnee Indian, who was killed in 1812 while in the service of the United States. His Indian name was Spemica Lawba, or High Horn. The town stands on the site of the old Miami town of Kĕ-nā-pē'-kwŏ-mă-kwa.

MACHESAW—Reservation made for a Potawatomi of this name by the treaty of 1832. The Potawatomi pronunciation is Măt'-chis-saw, and the meaning is Bleating Fawn.

MANHATTAN—Postoffice in Putnam County, named from Manhattan Island, New York. The meaning is uncertain, because the original form of the word is unknown. The old Dutch writers called it Manatte, which resembles the Delaware "menatey," meaning an island. Heckewelder says it is a corruption of manahachtanienk, and means "the place where we all got drunk." Schoolcraft derives it from manau, meaning "bad," and atun, "a channel," with the terminal locative; and says the reference is to Hell Gate. Tooker makes it "island of hills." Other translations are "small island," "beautiful view," and "place where wood is gathered for bows and arrows." The last refers to a growth of hickory said to have been on the island. The chances favor Heckewelder's view, as Manhattan was not originally an island, for the Harlem and Spuyten Duyvel Creek were not connected at low tide.

MAJENICA—Postoffice in Huntington County; also creek. They are named for the Miami chief Mŏn-jē'-ni-kyah, which means "big body," or rather "big frame," for it refers to the size of the entire person.

MAKKAHTAHMOWAY—Common form of name of a Potawatomi chief who had a joint reservation with Menominee at Twin Lakes, in Marshall County. The name is pronounced Mă-kah'-tă-m'wah—the final syllable varying to m'wĕh—and the meaning is "Black Wolf."

MANITOU—Lake in Fulton County. This is the Potawatomi mă-nē'-tō—the Miami form being mah-năt′-o-wah—and refers to a supernatural monster said to inhabit the lake. Mă-nē′-tō signifies merely a spirit, and good or bad qualities are indicated by adjectives.

MAUMEE—River of northeast Indiana, tributary to Lake Erie. The name is a corruption of Mē-ah′-mē, approaching the Indian pronunciation, and abandoning the French spelling. It was formerly called "the Miami of the Lake," and still earlier as the Ottawa River, on account of the residence of that tribe on its banks. John Johnston gives "Cagh-a-ren-du-te, or Standing Rock," as the Wyandot name of the stream. This name refers to a large rock near the foot of the rapids, known as Roche de Bout.

MARAMECH—One of the bands or divisions of the Miamis. It is the Peoria word for "catfish," sometimes written maramek, or maramak. The Miami form is mē-ăl′-lō-măk, sometimes written malamak; and the Potawatomi and Odjibwa forms are man-amak, or manumaig. The term "Miamis of Maramech" refers to their location, probably on a stream of that name, of which there were several. The most important was the Kalamazoo, of Michigan, on which these Indians lived for some years. They were probably the same band as those later known as "Eel Rivers."

MAXINKUCKEE—Lake in Marshall County. The name has been written in various ways. The Potawatomi pronunciation is Mŏg-sin'-kēē-ki, and the meaning is "Big Stone Country." There were several terminal moraines about the lake, which have made extensive rock bars in it. Many of the bowlders that formerly lay on the shores have been gathered up and used for foundations and retaining walls. Old fishermen claim that there is one enormous bowlder in the south end of the lake that comes within five or six feet of the surface of the water, and is an especially good fishing place; but it is rare that any of them can locate it.

MAZAQUA—Reservation in Cass County, to a Miami chief whose name appears in various forms but is properly pronounced Mē-zē'-kwah. It is their word for hail or hailstones.

MEMOTWAY—Reservation for band of a

Potawatomi chief of this name, on the Tippecanoe River in Fulton County. It is
pronounced Mĕh'-mŏt-way, and is the
name of the catbird. Literally it means
"complaining," or "crying out from pain,"
the reference being to the querulous note
of the bird.

MENOMINEE—Potawatomi reservation in
Marshall County, and village in same at
Twin Lakes, where there was a Catholic
mission. Mē-nŏm'-i-nē means "Wild Rice
People" and was applied to the tribe of
that name on account of their extensive
use of wild rice for food. The Miamis
call wild rice nay'-lō-min, or wild grain,
but the Potawatomis use mē-nŏm-in.

MESHINGOMESHIA—Miami reservation on
the Mississinewa River in Wabash and
Grant counties, and village in Grant
County. The name is Mē-shing'-gwă-
min'-ji, but it occurs in numerous forms,
and is popularly corrupted to "Shingle
Mash." Specifically it is the name of the
burr-oak tree, and is often used as a personal name for both males and females.
Min-ji, in composition, means "tree." The
remainder of the word may be a survival

of a primitive Algonquian form, corresponding to the Delaware m'chingwe, and meaning "large;" or it may be "shinggwah," meaning "leaves," which is used by the Miamis in composition, although they use shē-pah-kwah as a separate word. The burr-oak is the largest of our oaks, with the largest leaves, and is a fine shade tree.

MESQUABUCK—Reservation at Tippecanoe Lake, in Kosciusko County, and village which stood at the site of Oswego, both named for the Potawatomi chief to whom they belonged, and who is popularly remembered in the vicinity as "Squaw Buck." The name is Mĕs'-kwah-bŭk, which is the Potawatomi name for "copper," and is sometimes used for red pipestone. Topash says it is also used to signify the red color of the sky at sunrise or sunset, and that it was applied to this chief in this sense.

METEA—Postoffice in Cass County named for the Potawatomi chief Mē'-tē-ah—McCoy calls him Meteor. His village was on the St. Joseph's, about nine miles above Ft. Wayne, at the mouth of Cedar Creek, and

ME-TE-AH (KISS ME.)

(From Portrait formerly in National Gallery.)

was called Mŭs-kwah'-wah-sē'-pe-ō'-tăn,
or Cedar Creek Town. Accounts of him
will be found in Keating's Narrative of
Major Long's Expedition in 1823; in Mc-
Kenney and Hall's Indian Tribes; and in
local histories of Allen and other counties.

METOSANYAH—Reservation and creek in
Wabash and Grant counties. The name
is commonly abbreviated to Tō-săn'-yăh,
and has been corrupted to Josina. It is the
exact equivalent of our new-coined word
"Amerind," i. e., American Indian. Literally, and no doubt originally, it means
"the Living," but after the coming of the
whites it would naturally be applied to
that portion of "the living" that were native to America. It is often used as a personal name for both males and females,
and is translated "Indian."

MIAMI—County, town, several townships
and streams all named for the Miami nation of Indians. The proper pronunciation is Mē-ah'-mē—in the plural Mē-ah'-
mē-ah'-ki, or Mē-ah'-mē-ŏk—but it is
hopelessly corrupted to Mi-ăm'-mi. The
Miamis do not know the meaning of the
word, and it is never translated by the old

chroniclers; so it is evidently a name given by some other tribe. The oldest forms given by the French writers are "Oumiamiouek," "Oumiamiak," etc. This is most probably "Wemiamik"—the Delaware name of the Miamis given in the Walum Olum. It means "all beavers," or "all beaver children," i. e., figuratively "all friends." The Delawares were on very friendly terms with the Miamis from the most ancient known times; and they called themselves "grandfathers" of all the Algonquian tribes. It has been urged that "Miami" is from the Odjibwa name of the tribe, "O-maum-eeg, or People who live on a peninsula," but there is no record that the Miamis ever lived on a peninsula, and it is more probable that this is an Odjibwa corruption of "Oumiamiouek," with a merely accidental meaning. An ingenious extension of this theory was based on the occurrence of the name "Miami" in Florida, originally applied to Lake Okeechobee, and later to a river and town on the east coast; but there is no evidence that the Miamis ever lived in Florida, and no probability that any Indian tribe would call Florida a peninsula. The Florida "Miami" is no doubt a corruption of "Mayaimi," the name of one of the ancient tribes of that region. The Miami nation included the tribes known as Ouiatanons, Piankeshaws, Twightwees, Eel Rivers, and, at an earlier date the tribes known as Illinois. See these names; also "Maramech." LaPotherie says of the Miamis: "They travel but rarely by water, but are great walkers, which has given them the name of Metousceptinioueks or pilgrims."

MICHIGAN—Lake and city. Michigan is probably of Odjibwa origin; compounded of mi-shi, meaning "great," and sa-giegan, meaning "lake."

MISHAWAKA—Town in St. Joseph County. The name is a corruption of the Potawatomi m'shĕh'-wah-kēk, a contraction of m'shĕh'-wah-kēē'-ki, or "country of dead trees;" in our common phrase "a deadening." There was at this point a tract of dead timber, caused by fire or storm.

MISHIKINOQKWA—Miami name of the celebrated Little Turtle; also his village on Eel River, sometimes called Turtle's Town. The pronunciation is Mi'-shi-kin-ŏq'-kwa

—the "q" representing a sound of "gh" similar to the German "ch." The literal meaning is "Great Turtle's Wife," but specifically it is the name of the painted terrapin (*chrysemys picta*), which is the commonest of the turtle family in this region. It is also the most gaudily colored, which explains the literal name, The Great Turtle being the chief beneficent deity of the Algonquian tribes. As the painted terrapin is small, not growing over six or eight inches across, the early interpreters, who did not know a special name for it, called it "the little turtle," and the name has become permanent.

MISSISSINEWA—Tributary of the Wabash, emptying at Peru. The name is also sometimes given to a Miami town at its mouth, otherwise known as Osage town. The Miami name is Nă-mah'-chis-sin'-wi, which as applied to the stream is translated "much fall in the river." Literally it means an ascent, or, as one mixed-blood explained it, "a consider'ble slope up, but not as much as a hill." It is formed from the verb nă-mah'-chis-sing, meaning "it slants." The name was formerly written, as it is still commonly pronounced in the neighborhood, Măs-sis-sin'-ē-way.

MODOC—Postoffice in Randolph County, named for the tribe of northern California which achieved notoriety by the massacre of the lava beds. It is said that the name was given to them by the hostile tribe of the Shasteecas, and that it means "enemies."

MOHAWK—Postoffice in Hancock County, named for the Iroquois. The meaning is uncertain, but is supposed to be "cannibal," as that interpretation was given it in 1676, when they were mentioned as "Maugwawogs, or Mohawks, i. e., man-eaters."

MONON—Postoffice and township in White County; also creek tributary to the Tippecanoe. Mō'-nŏn is a Potawatomi word exactly equivalent to "tote," as used in the South. If you carry anything the act is monon. If you accompany a person it is monon. If you drive one's carriage, or take him in your own, it is monon.

MOTA—Reservation and town of a Potawatomi chief in Kosciusko County. The name is pronounced mō'-tay, and means a jug, or a big bottle.

Mukkonsqua—The celebrated captive
Frances Slocum was named Mŭk-kōns′-
kwă by the Miamis. The name means
Little Bear Woman.

Mukkose—Potawatomi reservation and village in Marshall County. The name has
been corrupted to Muckrose, Maukose,
Mankekose, etc., but is properly Mŭk′-
kōse. It is a diminutive form, meaning
Little Beaver.

Muncie—County seat of Delaware County,
originally known as Munseetown or Mun-
ceytown. It was so called because there
was a large town of the Delawares, mostly of the Munsee or Wolf clan, on the
north side of the river at this point. Mŭn-
see is a corruption, developed through
Monsey, and Monthee, from Mĭn′-si or
Mĭn′-thiu, meaning "People of the Stony
Country," and referring to their former
mountainous home in the East. They were
commonly called Loups, or Wolves, by
the French. The Delaware name of this
town was Wah′-pi-cŏm-ē′-kōke, or Wah-
pi-kah-mē′-kŭnk, which means White
River Town. It was the easternmost of the
Delaware towns on White River—the

first reached by the trails from the north, east and south,—and took this name by pre-eminence. The town originally stood a short distance farther up the river; and it is said in local histories that it was then called "Outainink," and that this means "Old Town." This is evidently due to a misunderstanding of the Delaware word utĕn-ink, which means "site of the town," or "place where the town was," but has been mistaken for the name of the town that was there.

MUSCACKITUCK—River of southern Indiana, tributary to the east fork of White River; often improperly written Muscatatack. Chamberlain says of it: "In Indian Mesh-caque-tuck or Pond River, from its many stagnant places in low water." This is erroneous. There is no such Indian word for "pond." There are no "stagnant places" in the Muscackituck even now, and it was a larger and steadier stream, when the Indians knew it, before the forests were removed. The ending "tuk" or "hit-tŭk" is never applied to stagnant water, and of itself implies water in motion. The name is Delaware—compounded of mŏsch-ăch'-geu, meaning "clear," "not turbid," and hit'-tŭk, meaning a stream—usually a small and rapid river. Hence, Mŏsch-ăch'-hit-tŭk—the "ch" sounded as in German—or Clear River.

MUSKELONGE—Lake in Kosciusko County, four miles south of Warsaw. There has been much discussion as to the proper form of the word—muskellonge, mascallonge, maskinonge, etc.—which is due to different dialects—the Odjibwa and cognate tribes having no "l," and substituting "n" for it. Its meaning is the same in Indian as in English—or literally "the great pike."

NANCY TOWN—Common name of Delaware village on White River, about 9 miles west of Anderson (S. E. 1-4 of Sec. 5, Range 7 E.). It was also known as Nantico, but properly as Nantikoke, being named for James Nantikoke, who lived there. Nantikoke is the name of one of the Delaware sub-tribes, and, according to Brinton, means "tide-water people," referring to their ancient residence between Chesapeake Bay and the ocean.

NAPPANEE—Town in Elkhart County, named for the Canadian town, which, however, is spelled with one "p." The name is the word for "flour" in the language of the Missisauga Indians, who, according to their chief Paudäsh, are a branch of the Shawnees, who were driven north from the Ohio Valley by the Iroquois. The Canadian name refers to a grist mill built in early times at the falls of the Napanee, or Apani River.

NASWAWKEE—Reservation in Marshall County, bordering Lake Maxinkuckee. The hill rising from Maxinkuckee landing is still known as Năs-waw′-kēē's Hill, the Government having built him a house there. The common spelling varies from Naswaka to Neeswaughgee, but the Potawatomi pronunciation is Năs-waw′-kēē. It means primarily "a feather;" but also "a feathered arrow," or "one who feathers arrows." The portrait of this chief in the National Gallery was marked "Na-swa-ga (The Feathered Arrow)" and that is presumably the meaning intended in his name.

NEAHLONGQUAH—Common form of name of

reservation in Allen County. It is a corruption of Nay-wil'-lĕng-wŏn'-gah, which means "Four Wings." This chief was commonly known to the whites as "Big Legs."

NOTAWKAH—Potawatomi chief who shared the Menominee reservation, in Marshall County. The name means "he hears," or "he listens."

OKAWMAUSE—Reservation to a Potwatomi chief under the treaty of 1832. The name is pronounced O'-kō-mouse, and means "Little Chief."

ONTARIO—Postoffice in Lagrange County, named for the lake. Schoolcraft says that Ontario is a Wyandot word—originally "on-on-tar-io"—and that it signifies "beautiful hills, rocks, waters." He supposes it to be expressive of the feelings on getting the view of the lake from Cadaracqui.

OSAGE—Name commonly given to the Miami town at the mouth of the Mississinewa, on account of the residence there of an Osage Indian. He lived among the Miamis as a member of their tribe, and appears in their treaties as "Osage," or

"Osage the Neutral." The Miamis called him Wah-shah'-shie, which is their name for the Osage tribe.

OHIO—County, named for the river. La Salle wrote of the river in 1680, "the Iroquois call it Ohio, and the Ottawas Olighin-cipou." Ohio is an Iroquois exclamation signifying "beautiful." Olighin-cipou is apparently the same as the old Delaware name Allegewi-sipo, which probably means river of the Talegewi or Talega, a tribe with whom the Delawares were at war anciently. John Johnston says that the Wyandots called the river O-he-zuh, meaning "something great;" and that the Shawnees called it Kiskepila-sepe, or "Eagle River." Hough gives the Delaware name as "Palawa-the-pee, or Turkey River." On the oldest French maps, the Ohio, at its mouth, is marked Ouabouskiau, Ouaboustikou, or Ouabouskigou. These are dialect forms of Wah-bah-shik'-ki, the Miami name of the Wabash. The tribes of this region treated the Wabash as the main stream, and the Ohio as tributary to it; and the French followed their nomenclature until about 1750.

OSCEOLA—Postoffice in St. Joseph County, named for the celebrated chief of the Seminoles (Rebels or Wanderers). The name is that of the great "medicine drink" of the Creeks, of whom the Seminoles are an offshoot, and of the mixed military and religious ceremony in which it is used. The name is more properly ŏs'-y-ō-hŭl'-la, and is taken from a prolonged note, yō-hŭl'-la, that is used in the ceremony. The whites commonly call this drink "black drink," but the Creeks call it "white drink," from the froth on the black liquid. It is a decoction of the leaves of the cassena or yaupon (*ilex vomitoria*), which the whites call Appalachian, Carolina, or South Sea tea. A description of the ceremony will be found in Schoolcraft's Archives, Vol. 5, p. 266.

OSWEGO—Town in Kosciusko County at the outlet of Tippecanoe Lake. The name is Iroquois. Beauchamp says: "Os-we-go, Osh-wa-kee, Swa-geh, are among the forms of a well known name. It means 'flowing out,' or 'small water flowing into that which is large.' The name belongs to the river, but was applied to the lake by the Onandagas, in which case it meant the lake at Oswego." The Indiana town is on the site of the Potawatomi village of Mĕs'-kwah-bŭk."

OTSEGO—Township in Steuben County. The name is Iroquois, taken from the New York lake. Beauchamp says: "Ote-sa-ga is Otsego Lake, and traditionally is supposed to refer to a large stone at its outlet. In the last century the name also appeared as Os-ten-ha, which A. Cusick tells me is something about a stone. Cooper, in the preface to Deerslayer, says that the stone above mentioned still retained the name of the Otsego Rock." Cooper's story, the scene of which was about this lake, was an effective agency for making the name popular.

OTTAWA—The earliest known name applied to the Maumee River, on account of this tribe living on its banks. Ottawas, or its short form Tawas, is commonly said to mean "traders;" but Lamothe Cadillac, in his memoir of 1695, says: "I will say only that the word Outaouas signifies in our language Nation des Nez Percez, because they pierce the nose, where they attach a little stone, much embellished, which falls to the middle of the mouth, between the two lips." He further says that the Ottawas were divided into four tribes: "the Kiskakons, that is to say Queues Coupees;" "the Nation du Sable, thus called because their ancient residence was in a sandy country;" "the Sinago;" and "the Nassauakueton, that is to say the Nation of the Fork."

OUIATANON—This is the form to which the name of the old French post on the north side of the Wabash, just below Lafayette, finally settled after existing in at least "57 varieties." The title of the tribe of the Miamis, for which it was named, ranged from Ouaouiatanonouek to Ouias in the French, and from Wawijachtenokes to Weas in English. The pronunciation of the full name is Wah'-wē-ah'-tŭn-ŏng. It was the common Algonquian name of the Detroit River, and of Detroit. Schoolcraft derives it from "wa-we-a, a round about course; ah-tŭn, a channel; and ŏng, locality." Our tribe probably took its name

SITE OF POST OUIATANON

from the Detroit River, for, in 1687, Du-
rantage speaks of "the Shawnees and Miamis, for a long time proprietors of the
said country of the Detroit River and Lake
Erie, from which they had retired for some
time for their greater utility;" i. e., to La-
Salle's colony on the Illinois. The name
is probably not of Miami origin, for in
their language wah'-wē-ah appears to be
restricted to the meaning "round," while
"curved" or "crooked" are denoted by
wah-kăkwh'; thus the full moon is wah-
wē'-ah-sit, i. e., "the round one," and the
crescent moon is wahk-shingh'-wah, i. e.,
"lying crooked." Post Ouiatanon was located in the west half of the east half of·
Sec. 27, Tp. 23 N., R. 5 W. The site
is crossed by the east and west center line, part lying in the N. E.
quarter and part in the S. E. quarter. It
is immediately west of a ravine and dry
run, which separates it from Sand Ridge
Church and cemetery. Excavation on the
east side opened the mixed French, Indian and British burial ground of the fort,
a number of relics from which are preserved at Purdue University. The local

D. A. R. has unfortunately put up a memorial tablet about a quarter of a mile from the real site. The Indian town was on the south side of the river, a little lower down, on what is now called Wea Prairie.

Owasco—Postoffice in Carroll County. The name is Iroquois, taken from the lake in New York, and is said to mean "floating bridge."

Patoka—River in southwestern Indiana, tributary to the Wabash; also town and island in Gibson County, and township in Pike County, named for the river. The river is said to have been named for a Musquakie or Fox chief, who lived in the vicinity more than a century ago. There is a postoffice and township of the same name in Marion County, Ill. There is record of a Fox chief in Illinois whom the whites called Patoka, but the Indians say the name is properly Pah-tă'-kō-tō (Pa-ta-go-to; Pat-a-ca-to). He was also called Tah-nă'-kō-mē, and was of the Wolf clan, to which the name Pah-tă'-kō-tō refers. Mr. W. C. Kohlenberg, superintendent of the Sac and Fox agency, writes of the name: "It refers to the height of the water on the side of a wolf in crossing a stream. In others words, they say it almost asks the question, of a wolf, 'How high did the water come upon you in wading across the stream?' Mr. (Henry C.) Jones is one of the best interpreters we have, but he is unable to give any other meaning." On this basis Patoka may be translated "How deep?" and the great fluctuations of the stream would make the name quite appropriate. I think, however, the name is a reference to some Comanche slave, as these were quite common among the Illinois Indians. The French called them Padoucas—a slight corruption of the common Algonquian term for them. In some old French chronicles it is Padocquia. The Miami form of this word for Comanche is Pah-tō'-kah.

PERU—The site of this city was called by the Miamis ik'-kē-pis-sin'-noong, or Straight Place, because the Wabash at this point is straight for about two miles.

PIANKESHAW—A tribe of the Miamis, whose chief towns were on the Vermillion River. In 1731, part of them, under the influence of Sieur de Vincennes, went with him to his new post, and established the village known as Chip-kah'-ki, or Chip-kah'-ki-oon'-gi. The meaning of Piankeshaw is uncertain, but Godfroy says that the idea it conveys to him is of something scattered about the ears. The Miami pronunciation is pē-ŭng-gish'-ah.

PIPE CREEK—Stream in Cass County, and township named for the stream. This is a literal translation of the Miami name of the stream—Pwah-kah'-nah—a pipe for tobacco.

PINJEWAII—Miami name of Jean Baptiste Richardville, their last head chief. The "n" of the first syllable is nasal—the pronunciation being Pin-jē'-wah. It was originally the name of the wildcat, but is now commonly used for the domestic cat. He was a half-breed, his father being a scion of the noble French house of Drouet de Richardville, and his mother Tah-kŭm-wah (On the Other Side—i. e., in place), a sister of Little Turtle.

PONCEAU PICHOU—Handed down as the name of Wildcat Creek, a tributary of the Wabash. It is an American corruption of Panse au Pichou, the French name of the stream, which is a literal translation of the Miami name Piⁿ-jē'-wah-mō'-ti, or Belly of the Wildcat. The name is often written Ponce Passu in local histories. On old French maps it is commonly marked Riviere Panse, a la Panse, or de la Panse.

POTAWATOMI—One of the most numerous of the Indiana tribes. Keating gives the pronunciation as Pŏ-tă-waw-tō'-mē, and says it means "we are making a fire," but Quashma gives me the pronunciation as Pō-tă'-wŏt-mē. The name is probably from the Odjibwa, Po-da-wand-um-eeg, or those who keep the fire. The Potawatomis, Odjibwas and Ottawas were very closely related, if not originally one people, and called themselves "The Three Fires." The Miami name of the Potawatomis is Wah-hō'-na-hah, but they often use the nickname, Pō-tŏsh'. The French nicknamed them Pous (French for lice), but the meaning is accidental, and the name merely an abbreviation, as the French made the first syllable of their full name "Pou." The Potawatomis became largely intermixed with other tribes at an early date, especially with the Sauks and Foxes.

PROPHET'S TOWN—Indian town on the north side of the Wabash, below the mouth of the Tippecanoe, at which Tecumtha and The Prophet gathered their followers. The Indian name of The Prophet has many dialect variations, due to his association with so many tribes. Mr. Frank A. Thackeray, superintendent and special agent at Shawnee, Oklahoma, writes me: "The brother of Tecumseh (The Prophet) is best known among the Shawnees by the name of Tems-kwa-ta-wa. The meaning of this word is 'one who keeps open door.'"

RACCOON—Big Raccoon Creek is a stream of western Indiana, tributary to the Wabash. On Hough's map it is marked Cheque-ak, which is evidently intended for the Miami nickname Chĕ'-kwi-ah, or Shĕ'-kwi-hah. They say this means "a poor 'coon," but can give no intelligible reason for it. The Miami word for raccoon is ă-say'pon. Kil-sō-kwă thinks that Shĕ-kwi-hah has some relation to shĕ'-kwa-tah, or taking marrow out of bones. The Indians used to crack bones, and extract the marrow for food.

ROANOKE—Town in Huntington County. The name is the word of the Virginia Indians for the shell money anciently used by them. It was sometimes written "roenoke;" and Capt. John Smith wrote it "rawrenock."

ROCKPORT—County seat of Spencer County. In Cockrum's Pioneer History of Indiana (p. 174) is given the statement of Joel Harden, who was carried captive from Kentucky by a mixed party of Kickapoos and Delawares, that the name of the site of Rockport "was Yellow Bank—in the Kickapoo language Weesoe Wusapinuk." There is some confusion in this. Weesoe Wusapinuk is Delaware instead of Kickapoo, and "Yellow Bank" was at Owensboro, eight miles below Rockport. The site of Rockport was called by the whites "Hanging Rock," from a projecting rock formation, now removed, that was sometimes known as "Lady Washington's Rock."

RUSSIAVILLE—Town in Howard County. The name is a corruption of Richardville, which was the French name of Pⁿ-jē-wah, the last head chief of the Miamis. The name Richardville was commonly pronounced, and often written, Rŭsh'-er-ville. The county was originally named Richardville, for this chief, but the name was changed to Howard in honor of Gen. Tilghman Howard.

St. Josephs River—The principal tributary of Lake Michigan from northern Indiana and southern Michigan. The Potawatomis, in whose country it was, call it Sahg'-wah-sē'-bē, which may be translated "Mystery River." Sahg'-wah is practically equivalent to our term "mushroom growth" or "spontaneous growth," i. e., something that springs up without any known seed. Topash says that the name came from a Potawatomi legend of a strange Indian, who was found on the bank of this stream, and no one ever learned who he was, or whence he came. Hence they called him Sahg'-wah, and gave this name to the stream.

St. Josephs River—The north branch of the Maumee. Kilsōkwă says that the Miami name of this stream is Kō-chis'-ah-sē-pē, or Bean River.

St. Marys River—The south branch of the

Maumee. John Johnson said that the Shawnee name of this stream was Coko-theke sepe, or Kettle River. On Hough's map it is marked Ke-ke-ong-se-pe—evidently a corruption of Ki'-ka-kŏn-sē'-pē. See Kekionga. The Miami name is Mah-may'-i-wah-sē-pē'-way, or Sturgeon Creek, the reference being to the fact that the sturgeon formerly resorted to the Maumee and its tributaries in great numbers in the spawning season.

SALAMONIE—Tributary of the Wabash, emptying opposite La Gro. The spelling is diverse—ranging from Sallimany and Solimony to Salamonia in the name of a town in Jay County which is named for the stream. The Miamis call the stream O-sah'-mō-nēē. Both this and the American name are corruptions of ōⁿ'-sah-lă'-mō-nee, the Miami name of the blood-root (*sanguinaria Canadensis*). Literally the word means "yellow paint"—from ōⁿ'-sah-wĕk—yellow (inanimate), and lă-mō-nee—paint. The plant is so called because the Indians made a yellow paint or dye from it. The name is identical with that of the Miami chief who lived opposite its mouth, and whom the French called Le Gros. He may have been named from the stream, or the stream from him.

SHANKITUNK—Stream in Rush County, tributary to Flat Rock. If the name is not much corrupted it means "Woody Place," from the Delaware tchanigeu, meaning "woody," and the terminal locative. Possibly, however, it is corrupted from tchăng-hit-tŭk, which would mean "Woody Creek."

SHAWNEE—Creek, township and prairie in Fountain County, named for the Indian tribe, a band of which lived in that vicinity, having a town at or near the village of Shawnee in Tippecanoe County. They were probably Chartier's band, which moved to that region from the Allegheny, in 1745. The name of the tribe, in all the Algonquian dialects, means "Southerners." The Miami form is shah-wahn'-wah.

SHEPAHCANNAH—The Miami husband of Frances Slocum, and the name of his village on the Mississinewa. Shē-pah'-kăn-nah is the name of the awl used by the Miamis in sewing skins—an instrument five or six inches long, made of metal, bone, or hard wood. In his later years Shē-pah'-căn-nah lost his hearing, and was thereafter commonly known as Kă-kip'-shah, or "Deaf." For this reason his village was commonly known to the whites as "The Deaf Man's Village."

SHIPSHEWANA—Postoffice in Lagrange County, also creek and lake, named for a Potawatomi Indian. Topash says it is a corruption of Shŭp'-she-wah'-nō, and means" Vision of a Lion." Shŭp'-shē probably meant originally a fierce beast with a large head and mane, and is now applied specifically to the lion. Wah'-nō is the name given to any vision seen after a "medicine fast."

TATAPACHSIT—The head chief of the Delawares, otherwise known as "The Grand Glaize King," who was executed for witchcraft in 1806; also the village on White River in which he lived. The name occurs in numerous forms, such as Talapoxie, Telipockshy, Teta Buxika and Tedpachksit. Heckewelder has it sometimes Tetepachski, and sometimes Tatapachkse, and Luckenbach Tetepachsit. It is identical with the old Pennsylvania treaty sig-

nature of "Tatabaugsuy or The Twisting
Vine;" but there is nothing in the name
approaching the Delaware words for
"twisting" or "vine." Literally "tata" is
an emphatic negative, and the verb pŏch'-
ŏn means to divide by force, or pull apart.
Such a name would not be given to any
frail vine, and the one notably twisting
woody vine of the Delaware country is the
American Woodbine (*lonicera grata*), of
which Tatapachske, or Tatapachsit, is
presumably the specific Delaware name.

TECUMSEH—Postoffice in Vigo County,
named for the celebrated Tecumtha. The
name means "going across," or "crossing
over." The common interpretations of
"a comet," "a shooting star," "a panther
leaping on its prey," etc., are probably
derived from illustrations of the meaning.

THORNTOWN—Town in Boone County, on
site of old Indian village at the center of
"the Thorntown Reserve" of 1818, which
was relinquished in 1828, and the Indians
removed to Eel River. The Miami name
of the Indian town and the reservation was
Kah-wē-ŏk'-ki-oong, i. e., Place of Thorns
or Thorn town.

TIPPECANOE—River, tributary to the Wabash; also postoffice, lake, county, and townships named for the river. The Miami name of the stream is Kē-tăp'-kwŏn, the name of the buffalo fish, which was formerly abundant, and is still common in the river and its tributary lakes. McCoy gives the Potawatomi form as Kē-tăp'-e-kŏn. Our word "Tippecanoe" is a corruption of Kē-tăp'-ē-kŏn-nŏng (i. e., Ketapekon town, or place), the name of the Indian town below the mouth of the river. "Canoe" is not a word of the North American Indians. There was a band of Miamis whom the French called "Tepicons," and this is probably a corruption of the name of the river.

TOPEAH—Reservation in Allen County, to Miami chief commonly known as Francois Lafontaine. The Miami pronunciation is Tō'-pi-ah, and Kilsokwa says it means "Frost on the Bushes," or Leaves.

TOPEKA—Postoffice in Lagrange County, named for the city in Kansas. The word is commonly said to mean "potatoes," or, as Kansas jesters allege, "small potatoes." This is indefinite as applied to Indian foods. The Kansas Historical Society adopts Dunbar's explanation that it is the Shawnee name of "the root of a species of sunflower found on the lowlands of the Kansas River." The only native plant answering to this description is the Jerusalem artichoke (*halianthus tuberosus*), the tuberous roots of which were a common food of the Indians, wherever found.

TRAIL CREEK—A tributary of Lake Michigan, emptying at Michigan City. This name, and the French name, Riviere du Chemin, are translations of the Potawatomi name, Mē-ĕh'-way-sē-bē-way. The old Indian trail from Niles to Chicago followed this stream.

TWIGHTWEES—Commonest form of the name given by the English to the Miamis living about Fort Wayne. The English took the word from the Iroquois, and its original form was Twich-twich,—"ch" sounded as in German—or Twigh-twigh. This is very like the word for "snipe" in some of the Iroquois dialects, and may have been adopted by them in derision of the crane totem of the Miamis, to which this band belonged. On the other hand, Godfroy informs me that "the other Indians, especially the Southern Indians, called the Miamis Tō-wă'-tō-wăs," but with what meaning he does not know. Brinton suggests that the name is the Delaware ta-wa (naked), repeated for emphasis; but there was no reason why the Miamis should be called naked by anyone, and especially by the Delawares, who were their friends. Possibly the name arose from the fact that the Ottawas, who were commonly called "Tawas," resided at the same place before the Miamis, and the Iroquois name may have been corrupted from this.

VERMILLION—River, tributary to the Wabash, and county named for the river. Colonel Croghan says that the stream was "so called from a fine red earth found there by the Indians, with which they paint themselves." On Hough's map the Indian name is given as "Osanamon," which is an Algonquian name of vermilion paint. Schoolcraft says it is compounded of "osawa—yellow," and "unimun," a plant from which the Indians made a red dye. This accounts for the French name of the stream—"Vermillon Jaune"—or "Red-Yellow" which exactly translates the Indian name, and very well describes the color. The National Board of Geographical Names undertook to "reform" the spelling of this word by dropping one "l," but as the spelling is established by the Indiana law creating the county it cannot legally be changed in this way. Our Miamis now do not use the word "osanimun," but call vermilion "lă-mō'-nēē, which is the general word for "paint," or sometimes nă'-pē-kŏng-lă-mō'-nēē, which means "red paint."

WABASH—The principal river of Indiana, with county, city and townships named for it. The name is a contraction of the Miami name of the stream, which is Wah-bah-shik-ki', or as more commonly pronounced, wah-pah-shik'-ki—"b" and "p" being convertible in the Miami, as in most Algonquian languages. The name is an inflection of the Miami adjective "white," which in its simplest (inanimate) form is wah-pēēk'. Wah-bah-shik-ki implies that the object to which it is applied is bright, or pure white, inanimate, and natural,

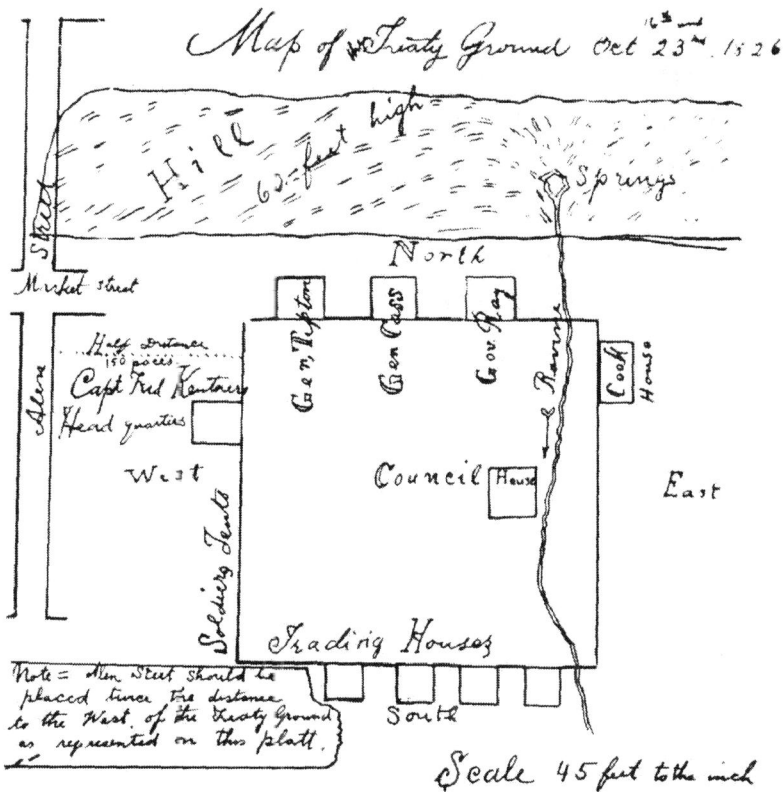

Map of ᴛʜᵉ Treaty Ground Oct 23ʳᵈ 1826

Hill 62 feet high

Springs

North

Street

Market street

Alun

Gen Tipton
Gen Cass
Gov Ray
Cook House

Half Distance
150 poles
Capt Fred Kentuck
Head quarters

Soldiers Tents

West

Council
House

East

Trading Houses

Note = Alun Street should be
placed twice the distance
to the West of the Treaty Ground
as represented on this platt.

South

Scale 45 feet to the inch

TAHKINGGAHMEOONGI.

Treaty Ground at Wabash.

such as a bright white stone, or shell. In
this case the name refers to the limestone
bed of the upper part of the stream. If
the noun qualified stood for something
artificial that was pure white, such as
cloth, or paper, the adjective form would
have to be Wah-pah-kin'-gi. The somewhat common theory that Wabash means
"a cloud driven by the equinoctial wind"
evidently originated from mistaking an illustration for a definition.

WABASH—County seat of Wabash County.
The Miami name of the location was Tah-
king-gah'-mē-oon'-gi, or "Running Water Place;" the reference being to a celebrated spring, variously known as Para-
dise Spring, Hanna's Spring and Treaty
Spring. The last name was given because
the treaty of 1826 was held here. The
spring was located about one hundred
yards west of the Big Four depot, on the
north side of Market street, but when the
street was improved the old spring was
closed, and the water piped across the
street to a drinking fountain. This is now
boxed up, and the water carried on to the
Big Four round house. The accompany-

ing map of the treaty grounds was made by Elijah Hackleman, who was familiar with them while the buildings were still standing.

WACO—Postoffice in Daviess County. The name, imported from Texas, is that of a sub-tribe of the Wichita Indians. It is pronounced way'-kō, and is sometimes writen in the Spanish form, Hueco. It is said to be their name for a heron.

WAKARUSA—Postoffice in Elkhart County. The name is imported from the West, being the same as Wau-ka-ru-sa, a stream in Kansas. It is commonly said to mean "hip-deep," but I have never found any statement of the tribal language to which it belonged.

WALUM CLUM—The chronological record of the Delaware Indians, obtained from those living on White River. The name is pronounced Wah'-lŭm O'-lŭm, and means "painted record."

WAPASEPAH—Reservation in Allen County. The name is a corruption of Wah'-pah-say'-pon, meaning White Raccoon. The Miami word for raccoon, ă-say'-pŏn, is obviously from the same original as its

Odjibwa equivalent aisebun, which School-craft derives from ais (a shell) and ebun (it was), giving a legend that the raccoon was made from a shell by the Great Spirit.

WAWASEE—Lake and postoffice in Kosciusko County, named for a Potawatomi chief. His grandson, Thomas Topash, who has the same Indian name, says it is pronounced Wah-wĕ-ăs'-sēē. It is the Potawatomi name of the full moon, and literally means "the round one." The name originally belonged to a small lake some five miles southwest of the present Walage; and the present Wawasee, which is partly artificial, being made by the dam at Syracuse which united several small lakes formerly connected by Turkey Creek, was known as Nine Mile Lake or Turkey Lake. The change was made by Col. Eli Lilly, who arranged with the railroad and postal authorities to name the station and postoffice Wawasee. Many of the people of the neighboring county still use the older names.

WAWPECONG—Postoffice in Miami County. The name is a corruption of wah'-pē-kōn, which means "white bone." The reason for selecting the name is not known.

WEA—Creek, postoffice and prairie in Tippecanoe County. The name is commonly pronounced wē'aw. The French form was ouia. These are abbreviations of Wah-wē-ah'-tung-ong, or Oua-oui-a-ta-non. See Ouiatanon. Godfroy says that the Wea village, which was located on the prairie, was called Wi'-ah-tŏn-oon'-gi, or Weah-tunong Town.

WESAW—Reservation and creek in Miami County, named for the Miami chief for whom the reservation was made. The word wē'-saw is the Miami name of the gall-bladder of an animal.

WHITE RIVER—The largest tributary of the Wabash, in central Indiana. It was originally in Miami territory, and their name for it is Wah'-pi-kah-mē'-ki, or "White Waters." The Delawares at first used the same name, varied in the Unami dialect to O-pee-co-me-cah, as the Unami use "ō-pēēk" instead of "wah-peek" for "white;" but later they commonly called the stream Wah-pi-hǎ'-ni, or "White River." On two of the oldest French maps White River is marked "Ouapika-minou" and "Oiapigaminou." These are evidently attempts at the Miami name, in which the engraver has mistaken the "k" of the final syllable for an "n."

WINAMAC—County seat of Pulaski County, named for a Potawatomi chief, whose name appears as Wenameac, Wenameck, Wynemac, Winnimeg, etc. This is the Potawatomi name of the catfish, derived from wēē'-nŭd, meaning "muddy," and măk, "a fish," indicating the preference of most species of catfish for muddy water. Winamac is a common Potawatomi name, and appears in the early French records as Ouenemek. The one for whom this town was named figured at the Fort Dearborn massacre as friendly to the whites, and was usually so, though he was said to have been with the hostiles at the battle of Tippecanoe. He made several visits to Washington, and died in the summer of 1821. There is a sketch of him in Thatcher's Indian Biographies.

WINNEBAGO—An Indian town on Wildcat Creek, destroyed by the troops under General Hopkins in 1812, named for the Winnebago tribe, which was quite largely represented among the followers of The Prophet. It contained "about forty houses, many of them from thirty to fifty feet in length, besides many temporary huts in the surrounding prairie." It was located on what is now known as the Langlois Reserve, adjoining the city of Lafayette. In our history it is often called Village du Puant, because the French called the Winnebagos "Puans," i. e., fetid. This name implies no reflection on the Winnebagos, who were cleanly enough, but refers to their river—Winnipeg, or Winnipeek,— which became offensively odorous in summer from dead fish. In fact Winnipeg may mean either "stinking water," "salt water," or "turbid water," and there has been a difference of opinion from the earliest times as to which was intended in the tribal name, with no prospect of its ever being definitely settled. Schoolcraft says that the Winnebagos call themselves Hochungara (Trout nation) or Horoji (Fish Eaters).

WINONA—Originally the name of a post-office on Bass Lake—otherwise known as

Cedar Lake—in Starke County, but now monopolized by the Winona Assembly for Winona Lake—formerly Eagle Lake—near Warsaw. The name is the same as the Wenonah of Longfellow's Hiawatha. Wi-nō'-nah is a Sioux, female, proper name, signifying a first-born child. If the first-born is a boy, the name given is Chăs'-kay, and in that case there can be no Winona in the family. When sex is not desired to be indicated the Sioux word for "first-born" is tō-kah'-pah, which is the numeral "first" and is also used as a comparative, meaning the elder or larger of two. In this sense it is the counterpart of hă-kah'-tă, which means the younger or smaller. The name Winona was first introduced to the reading public by Keating's pathetic account, in his Narrative of Long's Expedition, of the Sioux maiden who committed suicide because her relatives sought to make her wed against her will. Since then it has been a popular name for Indian girls with American writers.

WYALUSING—Stream in Jennings County, tributary to the east fork of White River. The name comes from Pennsylvania, where it is given to a small tributary of the Susquehanna. It was also the Delaware name of the Moravian Mission of Friedenshuetten (Tents of Peace) which was located near the mouth of this stream. As to the meaning, Heckewelder says: "Wyalusing Creek. M'chwihillusink (properly) is at the dwelling-place of the hoary veteran. An ancient warrior having resided on that creek about one mile above the town was the cause of this place being so named, in remembrance of him."

WYANDOTTE—Postoffice in Crawford County, and formerly one in Tippecanoe County. The latter adjoins what is known as the Richardville reservation, on which was located "The Wyandot Town" where the Miami treaty of 1828 was made. The name is from the tribe. Heckewelder says it was Ahouandate, but early chroniclers usually wrote it Yendat, or Wendat. Opinions differ as to the meaning, but Horatio Hale is probably right in his view that it means "People of One Speech." The French called these Indians "Hurons," referring to their hair, which they wore like the Ottawas in a bristling band across the head from front to back.

YELLOW RIVER—Stream in northern Indiana, tributary to the Kankakee. Brinton identifies this with the Wisawana (Yellow River) of the Walum Olum, but Rafinesque thinks the Wisawana was the Missouri. The Potawatomi name of the Indiana stream is Way-thŏw'-kah mik, which means Yellow Waters.

Massacres of the Mountains: a History of the Indian Wars of the Far West

BY JACOB PIATT DUNN

"Of the many volumes which have been written on our Indian wars, this of Mr Dunn is entitled to rank among the best, if not as the very best "—*The Critic*

' Mr Dunn's book has the great merit of sincere effort to bring the actual situation and the prejudices and habits of both sides into view "—*The Nation*

".A book which embodies a great deal of research, recounts much straightforward history, and furnishes enough of romance, tragedy and pathos to stir by turns the reader's interest, pity and indignation "—*The Literary World*

"It is a history—full, accurate, just and teeming with dramatic interest "—*Harper's Monthly*

Published by Harper & Brothers   Price $3 75   *For sale by all dealers*

Indiana: A Redemption from Slavery

(American Commonwealth Series)

BY JACOB PIATT DUNN

"The story is beautifully told Home life is represented Customs and dress and methods of labor are described We have a genuine history of the first people of that great region"—*Public Opinion*

"Mr Dunn has struck on the line of genuine interest and dignity, which runs through the history of the states formed on the soil of the Northwest Territory"—*N Y Independent*

"Excepting Prof Johnston's 'Connecticut,' we may pronounce this last volume the most scholarly of the series It certainly ranks in the very first grade"—*The Critic*

"It is a most interesting book;—all through it the reader's closest attention is gladly given"—*The School Journal*

"His volume is in every respect one of the most valuable of an exceedingly valuable series"—*Boston Traveler*

Published by Houghton, Mifflin & Co Price $1 25 For sale by all dealers

CPSIA information can be obtained
at www.ICGtesting.com
Printed in the USA
LVHW051949040323
740942LV00032B/1530

9 781016 186421